Preface

I've worked in the UK advertising industry for over forty years.

In mid-2013, I was delighted to be asked to pen a regular opinion column for MediaTel, and industry leader in online information for advertising media planners and buyers.

I was privileged for my outpourings to sit alongside those of the three leading journalists in the space : Raymond Snoddy, Dominic Mills and Torin Douglas. No competition, then.

I wrote in my capacity and from my perspective as a Director of ISBA, the organisation that represents British advertisers. Whenever I venture to express my own, and perhaps differing, opinions, I make it clear. MediaTel's editor's comments appear in *italics* throughout.

Two years on, and MediaTel tell me to my surprise that my columns are and continue to be well-read. Who am I to argue with digital turn-path data?

So I thought I would edit them into a compendium - hence this book. It's arranged in chronological order by month of publication and some months contain multiple topics.

I hope you enjoy reading it. And trust me, there's plenty more to come too...

Bob Wootton

London, February 2016

October 2013

Struggling to see the upside of the Publicis-Omnicom Group merger? Me too.

Bob Wootton is not short of an opinion or two, and having spent over 15 years lobbying and representing advertisers for ISBA and, before that, 20 years media buying for leading London agencies, where better to start his monthly column than the biggest media merger in history...

For some time I have been suggesting that the industry's next big competition battle will not be around a media owner consolidation, but an agency. It still came as a shock, though, when the Omnicom-Publicis mega merger hit the news, surely the biggest headline to hit the industry for some time, perhaps ever. Its impact all the greater from its suddenness when compared with that of WPP whose empire was built more gradually.

Tellingly, almost all the public reaction – a lot of it good, common sense, I might add – has been from independent commentators, be they non-aligned agencies or journalists, while the industry's leading lights noticeably taciturn even now, over two months since the news broke. Why?

Well, it's pretty obvious. The merger is so 'mega' that it impacts almost everybody. The industry bodies that represent advertisers (ISBA), agencies (IPA) and the whole industry (AA) are all, to some greater or lesser extent, conflicted.

The industry's leading lights are noticeably taciturn. Why?"

Unsurprisingly, ISBA, alongside many other parties, has been canvassing the views of its members and discussing the related issues iteratively with them and it is already clear that there may not be consensus among advertisers. Indeed, on the weekend of the merger announcement back in July, independent consultancy IDComms published an excellent piece suggesting that the top 20 global advertisers should expect some imminent and serious POG luuurve, but that the rest should take a cold, hard look at the implications for them.

Agencies too, are divided. You might expect competing agencies to fear and rail against the creation of such a massive competitor. But think again. If WPP is to regain its top spot, it doesn't want to make a competition referral which might scupper POG but also its own onward growth path too.

And if WPP does fight back as declared, one hell of an acquisition spree and a resounding 'kerching' could be on the cards for the remainder of the industry. Especially the 'Cinderella' networks and the stronger independents whose senior executives will doubtless jockey for senior positions in the emerging entities while they earn their way out to their fortunes or claim significant payoffs.

Following this logic, the only group we might expect to hear strong words from are the media owners, who surely have quite a bit to fear from the emergence of another truly massive media buying point. But, again, this ain't necessarily so; the media are still overwhelmingly local, by which I mean national, and while their voices may be loud in their individual territories and amongst the politicians who crave the publicity afforded by their channels and pages, they don't aggregate to a loud global voice.

ITV's Adam Crozier came out bullish, and in fairness he might have a point as he's already got a bigger worry in the UK; Group M is already >35% of UK media spend compared with POG's putative ~28%.

Very few people can see much, if any, upside for anybody except Publicis' and Omnicom's top management and shareholders."

Only the Googles and Facebooks (and the Newscorps!?) have that sort of scope. But while they are massive, they are also few. Though they should be concerned with the appearance of huge diversified agency networks with serious data, targeting, trading and aggregation capabilities of their own. Perhaps it even suits their highly-automated ways only to have two major customers to strike deals with?

(A point brought into sharper focus when bodies like the one I work for are reminding advertisers to insist on their right to free access to all anonymous data generated by and attendant to their media spends).

What is equally clear is that so far very few people can see much, if any, upside for anybody except Publicis' and Omnicom's top management and shareholders. I confess I'm in this camp myself. I foresee yet further consolidation, rising barriers to entry and reduction of choice. I don't buy the 'talent arguments' – most real talent I've met wants to control its own destiny and the online economy has made that far, far more possible.

Nor do I believe that either better media prices or the 'efficiency dividends' touted at every merger (in this case, an impressive $500 million) will find their way back to many clients, however large. A view corroborated by another good piece, this time from AdMath, which suggests that agency consolidation has not stemmed media inflation, at least not in the US.

The best hope most parties have is the interest of the competition authorities, most likely in the US or Brussels, but perhaps in some local markets like France too. But even then it will be a long haul.

November 2013

Social media sites pay heed...

I was dismayed when Facebook started showing decapitation videos again. Why does the social media giant continue to antagonise advertisers by directly refusing to give them safe passage on the channel?

I had intended my second Newsline column to be about transparency – an increasingly hot topic which would rather neatly coincide with ISBA's first Agency Commercial Issues event today (5th November). But that was until I learned via the BBC last month that Facebook had re-relaxed its rules concerning offensive/upsetting material on its pages.

As a result of this relaxation, a video originating from Mexico, purportedly showing a human decapitation, had appeared without warning. Some advertising for brands, including Zipcar, had also appeared alongside the video. Nissan, one of a number of major advertisers that suspended activity on Facebook in April after its ads had appeared in unacceptable surroundings, had subsequently returned to Facebook only to find themselves in the thick of things once again.

Within a day, even the Prime Minster David Cameron had weighed in, branding Facebook's policy "irresponsible". The next day, Facebook was reported to have capitulated and reinstated tighter rules.

This incident resurfaced a number of hot issues:

– The legitimate notion that a medium, particularly a social medium, should be a channel for free speech and expression.

– The responsibility and accountability, both to users and, where relevant, paying advertiser customers, which that freedom carries. "Hey, we're just a pipe" is simply not good enough.

– Recognition that these channels are global and that the audience within might have different standards, points of view, thresholds of offence and disgust and so on.

– The concept of advertiser 'safety', which I'll return to.

– And the way tech companies do business and deal with issues.

As the Facebook incident is the stimulus for this piece, most of my comments relate to it, though they also apply to other ad-funded tech companies.

Advertising follows audience. Advertisers seek to put their brands in places that will reach and persuade their target customers, existing or new. In most cases, those advertisers have invested enormous amounts of money over long periods of time to establish those brands and their values, whatever those might be.

Whilst there are a few advertisers who court controversy because it can be a cheaper, if also riskier, way of getting mass media coverage than buying it – think Ryanair or Paddy Power, for example – I've never met an advertiser who actively looks to appear in extremely contentious environments.

By contentious, I don't mean 'page three' or lads' mags, but seriously offensive/distressing things like hard porn, incitements to violence, rape, snuff...

There's a damn good reason for this. It's very bad for their brands.

The nature of internet advertising means that ads can be targeted and served in real time to individual users through some amazing tech. There are now literally billions of individual ad transactions going on every day.

Facebook has been in the midst of undertaking a review of its processes but it's very cagey on how this review is going. Could it be filibustering?"

In display this can lead and has led to some very unfortunate ad placements, which is why ISBA got together, initially under the IASH (Internet Advertising Sales Houses) initiative and latterly under the auspices of the Digital Trading Standards Group, to stem this where ever possible.

In the ad-funded social media like YouTube, Facebook, Twitter et al, this is a yet greater challenge because not only are the commercial messages being served atomically and in real time, but the content is being created thus as well.

The opportunity for slips when the transactions are in their billions means that an error rate of zero is probably impossible.

But that doesn't mean we can't and shouldn't be pressing the tech companies that have developed incredibly swift and clever algorithms and business models to serve their users and monetise the resultant audiences to repurpose these to protect their advertiser customers' brands.

Indeed, ISBA has been pressing Facebook and others to do so for some time. Characteristic of tech companies based (and setting policy) far away, and sometimes from a different starting perspective, it's been tough to engage. Only when certain advertisers got their fingers burnt and withdrew support was their attention really drawn.

Facebook has been in the midst of undertaking a review of its processes since July but it's very cagey on how this review is going. Could it be filibustering?

And then it decided to relax the rules it had previously tightened and what did we get? Decapitation. What does Facebook think it's up to? There are only two ways this can go – the slow way and the quicker way.

The slow way involves disenfranchising users so much that they migrate elsewhere. Carrying such distressing content might be 'edgy' to some, but it will likely be deterrent to many more. If audiences leave, the advertising model is depleted and a media company's value is destroyed. But as I say, this is a relatively slow process.

The (much) quicker road to ruin is to antagonise advertisers directly by refusing to give them safe passage in your channel, and that's what seems to be happening here.

Almost the entirety of Facebook's revenues comes from advertising in some form or other. That means the company's valuation is critically dependent on advertising revenues and prospects.

In this context, advertiser skittishness (what a polite word!) is something that should be avoided at all costs. The online social players should grasp this before it's too late, and the newcomers should learn from their elders' mistakes lest they too fall foul of it.

Until next time, when I promise transparency will be back on the agenda.

December 2013

Transparency at a premium in the digital age

Dominic Mills lit the flame and then VivaKi's Marco Bertozzi threw petrol on it; now, **ISBA's** *Bob Wootton speaks up for advertisers over the thorny issue of trading desks and transparency…*

Come closer to your screen dear reader, for today I'm going to talk dirty. Real dirty. You know – the 'T word'. Yep, transparency. The very mention of which gets people very twitchy, **as we saw last week**[i].

It's on the rise in many advertisers' minds right now. Why? A combination of a lot of different factors; almost a perfect storm, you might say.

Over the past year or so, an increasing number of the big brand owners ISBA represents and speaks for have been seeking our advice on how to respond to their agencies' requests for variations to their contract. These include:

– Proscribing which auditors the client can use to evaluate their media buying performance (media auditing to you and me) and their financial compliance with their contract (compliance auditing).

– Withdrawing the advertiser's rights to certain kinds of data, which in turn splits two ways – data thrown up as a consequence of a typically digital media buy, and data relating to the evaluation of an agency's media buying performance.

– And a third, closely related, seeks to ringfence what's being termed 'inventory media' (that's any media bought speculatively by the agency on its own account as opposed to being bought on behalf of clients) from scrutiny.

Ever since agencies started to do umbrella deals with media owners across all their clients and then charging the media out differentially so as to meet, but not exceed, their contracted obligation to each, they have effectively been broking. Clients have, by and large, gone along with it because it's delivered the results. But where does broking end and arbitrage begin?

As media channels proliferate, so deals become more complex and sources of normative pricing and value evaporate."

Then there's what's becoming known as 'digital shrinkage'. Digital media are usually billed on serving, not on viewing. And according to sources like Meetrics or comScore who, amongst others, offer tools in this space, only about 50% of ads appear in view. The rest are partly or completely out of view until the user scrolls to them, which they often don't.

Media and compliance auditors are also claiming that of every pound spent in digital media, the agency retains 50p, give or take. I use the term 'agency' here to include its trading desk, demand side platform, adserving, data management platform, and so on.

We've all dined out on the fantastically complicated LUMA/Improve Digital charts which show all the different types of digital company in the food chain. What isn't mentioned so often is the amount of cross-ownership between many of those companies.

Whatever happened to digital – the ultimately accountable, and therefore transparent, medium? It even makes out-of-home, long held under suspicion for its multiple commissions and volume overrider deals, look pretty clean. Ouch!

Some advertisers are reacting by going it alone with their own trading desk, some via a ringfenced unit within their agencies, some with a third party. But the jury's out on whether the benefits of greater visibility, transparency and control outweigh the downside of not being able to access all relevant inventory. I confess I haven't fully grasped this last bit. At least not yet.

Agency consolidation and the rise of holding group trading companies adds to the pressure. It's emerging that agency groups like to keep their agency and trading group people at some distance because it enables 'plausible deniability' on the part of the agency's client business directors.

There's a growing concern amongst advertisers that media agencies now 'plan the buy' to meet their deals, which include all kinds of ways to conceal incremental remuneration, instead of buying the most optimal media & communications plan for the brand.

Meanwhile, agencies are getting behind 'storytelling' across multiple channels, which plays well to their clients who are seeking better integrated execution of their brands' communications. As media channels proliferate – for example, new non-spot uses of TV – so deals become more complex and sources of normative pricing and value evaporate.

The whole business world is on a downward ratchet, so it's maybe naïve to expect advertisers to pay more."

But the pricing of a schedule of spots can easily be 'sweetened' to pass an audit with flying colours by loading the cost onto a sponsorship, product placement or a piece of advertiser-funded content. This raises significant challenges for media auditors.

Northern & Shell/Five proprietor Richard Desmond broke the industry code of omerta at the Cambridge TV convention a few weeks ago when he alleged that Five was over a barrel to carry content produced by Group M's entertainment arm, lest it was taken off the spot advertising schedule.

Beyond it being their money at risk, advertisers also have a key stake in this muddle. It might still have happened, but it wouldn't be nearly so widespread or run so deep had their procurement people not driven right into the ground the visible remuneration available to the agency.

Granted, agencies didn't have to keep shaving their rates to win new business at pitch. Or did they? So many of their business models are scale-based; the mantra being 'acquire volume at any cost and worry later'. The advent of dynamic, atomised media trading, real time bidding and, latterly, the need for the scale to work with data further exacerbate this.

To be fair, agencies are businesses too, particularly those in public ownership, and they exist to make money and turn profit. They're also populated by very bright, motivated and flexible people. No wonder a growing number have sought and found many ways of bolstering income invisibly – 21 at the last count, according to Anteus consulting.

The whole business world is on a downward ratchet, so it's maybe naïve to expect advertisers to pay more. But it's not too late for more collegiate conversations between clients and agencies as to each other's business needs from a relationship, and in turn a more sensible conversation about the proportionate distribution of the spoils – few of which would exist without the client having provided the 'risk capital' through their adspend.

There are some potentially positive developments.

IPA President Ian **Priest's ADAPT agenda for his two-year term**[ii] aims to create a more sensible conversation between advertisers and agencies. It's a laudable plan, though it seems a bit one-sided, at least at the moment.

There's a strong argument that advertising has never been that transparent. Indeed, back in the day, my agency was as culpable as the next in the field of production markups. But a lot has changed since then. The very term 'agency' is increasingly misleading – it implies that the client's best interests are paramount, when this is no longer necessarily the case.

So, if we're going to have a mature conversation around the IPA's call for a 'relationship contract', we'd better get all the issues on the table. Agencies may not make much progress while they are in denial about how they earn most of their money nowadays.

Meanwhile, WARC reports that a number of US agencies are now declining RFP's, which they consider uneconomic. The US Association of National Advertisers (ANA) is reported as welcoming this move – perhaps surprising, but in truth close to the money.

Following the success of the ANA model, which attracts several hundred delegates each year, ISBA ran its first Advertiser Commercial Issues conference recently and these issues were firmly on the table throughout. It certainly doesn't look like they're going away – quite the contrary in fact.

January 2014

Some good cheer for advertisers...and a bit of humbug

Back from the seasonal break, Bob Wootton shares his thoughts on mobile technology, the future of the BBC and fires a caustic shot across the bow of anyone unfortunate enough to have sent him an e-card this Christmas...

Spotify free goes mobile

Two weeks into January and I am still as excited and delighted as a six-year-old on Christmas morning. I've been grumbling for a couple of years, to anyone who would listen, about Spotify's only premium product being made available on mobile devices.

As a music fanatic, I've loved Spotify from day one, but I've always felt that Spotify Premium's £12 per month price tag was a bit steep. I know I used to spend way more than that on CDs – I'm just tight.

I held a strong suspicion it would get four times the subscribers if it halved its price, effectively doubling its revenues. It took me a (very) long time to figure out that maybe Spotify didn't want more Premium subscribers as it made more money from advertising on its free service.

Anyway, now it's announced that it's going to extend its free (that is, funded by ad interventions) service to mobile. Moreover, by the time I read the news and logged on it had actually extended the service, so it worked first time.

Good news for me and advertisers alike.

BBC eats itself

Not a week passes without further recriminations at the BBC. Savile; payoffs; directors general despatched in short order; BBC Trust Chairman Lord Patten clinging on for dear life, behaving like a cornered bear and scrapping like the seasoned politico he undoubtedly is.

All underpinned by the commonly held view that Auntie is a Byzantine organisation, as talented at cronyism and self-preservation as it should be at broadcasting.

And now we learn that it has unsurprisingly sent its first of many salvos to the Culture, Media & Sport Select Committee arguing for – you guessed it – preservation of its secure funding via a mandated universal tax known as the licence fee. There will be much more of this over the forthcoming months and years.

One of my first big briefs when I arrived at ISBA in 1996 was to get advertising on the BBC. At a time when the BBC took between a third and half of all the nation's viewing eyeballs, this made sense for advertisers seeking to defray the high cost of telly as sold by a few near-monopoly channels.

But this was not only a futile quest in the teeth of some of the most powerful lobbying opponents in the land. Events overtook me, not least the internet, the economy and a regulatory pricing intervention. As a happy corollary the price of TV advertising has not moved much since and represents the best in real terms for over a decade.

Meanwhile, advertisers have a choice of many, many channels (including some laden with BBC content) as well as enhanced sponsorships, product placements and digital extensions from websites to video on demand. Not to mention the multitude of new online routes to market and transaction.

So, thankfully, market forces have prevailed, everybody has seen sense and my futile objective has been abandoned.

But we still take a keen interest in the BBC because it is still a source of market distortion in programming, audience and, therefore, the broadcast economy. It's also a national institution and one which is fascinated by advertising. Hardly a week passes without some enquiry about advertising from the serried ranks of BBC newshounds; the volume of which makes you wonder whether downsizing had ever occurred.

Does its leadership hold the key? Seems to me there are pretty much three ways to run the BBC. Statutory regulation, which carries the threat of political interference. A Board of Governors, which so utterly discredited itself by cheerleading when it should have been overseeing, and the BBC Trust, a middle way that ISBA and many other commentators welcomed.

But that, too, has failed, and arguably more dramatically than its Governor Board predecessors. That leaves statutory control under Ofcom. Bring it on?

4G one year on

I got an iPhone 5 with 4G about a year ago. I had to migrate from long-time provider O2 to EE, who stole the march with their early 4G launch.

I thought I'd better have first-hand experience of something I was bound to be asked for an opinion on. Well, I would say that, wouldn't I? So, anticipating the question, here's how I've found it.

First impressions were mixed. Where I could get 4G it impressed immediately. I didn't have to duck into a Wi-Fi café every time I needed to update apps or download mail (useful for deleting unopened e-cards!) and media content while out and about.

Trouble was, it was really patchy and didn't follow any logic. One minute you'd be in 4G signal, the next 3G. Once I left central London, it was pretty hopeless.

I've also sensed, along with many I've spoken to, that 3G seemed to be performing (even) worse. Now, of course, I'd changed networks so there were too many variables for me to be able to isolate the cause. But true to their claims, week by week things improved and they're now pretty good most places I go. The premium for 4G over 3G isn't too punishing and is closing all the time. I recommend it if you hammer your smartphone like I do.

Bah, humbug

Finally, as you read this, many of you will have just returned from a (hopefully) well-earned Christmas break. I hope you had a really good one.

There, now I've officially spread some goodwill – and while the opportunity is still fresh – I'd like to have a mini-rant about Christmas cards, or rather the growing trend among us to eschew them for typically execrable jpegs or animated gifs along with the message that the money saved will be donated instead to 'cheridee'.

Am I the only curmudgeon who thinks that the giving of cards and donating to charity is not mutually exclusive? Here's a radical idea, let's do both – after all charity Christmas cards are not hard to find!

My inner Scrooge might prefer to send e-cards because it requires less effort and thought, and not because it frees up vital extra funding for our favourite donatable cause. But the Bob Cratchit that stirs in me around this time of year enjoys buying, writing and posting a real card that can be placed on an actual mantelpiece.

Personally, it was quite a lot of work lining up and signing several thousand business cards and a hundred or so personal ones, but it was part of what made it different, special. I may well be in a minority on this, and I'm sure some will consider me ungrateful or even heartless, but I assure you my heart's just in a different place.

Next year, I will be sending cards earlier and more widely than ever, maybe even with the exhortation that I'd quite like to receive one back and yes, I'm going to send all those wanky e-cards straight to junk without opening. Bah humbug indeed!

February 2014

The trouble with new tech is how democratising it all is

High-end audio visual chicanery is no longer the sole preserve of advertisers with the deepest pockets. Easily accessible tech has democratised content creation – but is this entirely for the good?

There will always be a place for visually stunning TV ads – the sort that stay in our collective memory for generations; you know, the ones that inspire deeply sincere grown-up dinner party conversation about the hidden symbolism in the imagery, the provenance of the artistic director, the backing track that will set a new musical genre.

There is no doubt that a powerful audio-visual experience can give a tired brand a useful shot in the arm – sometimes even a shot of adrenalin straight to the heart.

I love these mega-campaigns, but by their nature they're few and far between, and, on their own, insufficient to sustain the West End's phalanx of high-end production companies.

But between these creative feasts, London's creative agencies could snack on the more run-of-the-mill TV commercials. The sort that would inspire nothing more than sympathy if you admitted knowledge of their existence among sophisticated circles.

The trouble with all this new technology is how democratising it is.

Nicholas Lovell's book The Curve – How to Make Money in the Free World reminds us of the power that once lay in the hands of gatekeepers, but is now within the gift of almost all of us.

Lovell cites broadcasters and publishers as examples of manufacturing and distribution businesses, with content attached. Take away the manufacturing (e.g. printing) and control of distribution/fulfilment (circulation, broadcast), and the means to drive profit is greatly diminished.

Too much has already been written bemoaning how paper pounds are being replaced by digital pennies. But it bears repeating that the internet has meant the production of quality content is nowhere near as cost-prohibitive as it once was. And while this has allowed creativity to flourish, it has also had a rather wilting effect on certain parts of the once certain creative supply chain.

Once upon a time, it was nigh-on impossible to create a good-quality sound recording without visiting a professional studio. Then, a couple of decades ago, we began to see the phenomenon of 'homemade' music conquering the charts. This was in part due to a shift in musicians' and consumers' tastes towards electronic material created on instruments that did not require expensive acoustic spaces in which to be recorded.

So the days of artists holing up in massive, city-centre or country manor recording studios for months on end were numbered. There is now only one serious live sound studio of scale left in Soho, for example, and most around the world are in trouble.

I've believed for a long time that the same thing would happen in video, and now it has. Just as would-be record producers could create music in ProTools, Logic, Cakewalk, Cubase etc on their home PCs or laptops, so budding video producers now work in software like Adobe Premiere. And boy can they create.

This causes problems for the incumbent video production industry, itself a legacy manufacturing business with some massive sunken, fixed costs.

Not just high West End rents, but sophisticated image manipulation and computer-generated imagery kit. Not cheap!

Interesting that companies like Quantel, which was unsurprisingly once owned by ITV franchisee Carlton and made much of this kit in its heyday (e.g. Paintbox, Flame, Harry et al), also owned one of the biggest makers of sound mixing desks, Solid State Logic.

My **videographer son Cal**[iii] avers that some scenes in the recent second instalment of multi-million box office hit The Hobbit (The Desolation of Smaug) were shot on a $200 GoPro camera, not your usual megamoney Panaflex, Sony or whatever.

London creative agencies and West End production and post-companies find themselves facing change on an unprecedented scale because the great ideas they specialise in – and they can be great – have been paid for through massive production costs.

But as I've said, there's a sea change afoot. How will these ideas be funded as the production costs that once funded them collapse?

Advertisers seeking audiovisual solutions are reporting that if they brief a job as 'online display' it will often come back at a tenth of the price of a TV commercial, but far from a tenth of the quality. More like 95%. So why would you continue to pay several hundreds of thousands when you only need to pay a few tens? The scale really focuses the mind.

You might think that tradition of paying artists different rates for different usages could help unlock the puzzle, but it doesn't in the new democratised world. There are hardly any barriers to entry anymore.

Anybody can set themselves up as an artist, agency, editor, whatever. Even the arguments about the best talent clustering are breaking down, as we're seeing in Shoreditch. Sure, they still all gather together physically, but no longer necessarily under company/agency flags.

The legacy system also had its roots in the scale of audiences attached to each usage. Telly paid (much) better because the audiences were in their millions (and because the artists' union was once dominant). The distribution and accumulation curves might look rather different, but nowadays, the right material can reach vast audiences regardless of whether it is broadcast, streamed, viewed on a TV screen or a computer.

There will always be ideas that need extreme production values and inputs. As I say, I've always been a sucker for these. And as long as there are a few, they will be eminently distinctive and watchable, and could justify their high costs. The question is: how many of these are justified? Because it sure isn't nearly enough to carry the high-end production industry into a prosperous future.

An object lesson in hustings (non-) behaviour

Along with most of the industry's great and good, I attended the Ad Association's packed, interesting and balanced half-day Lead 2014 event. The standout, from a news perspective, was the three breakout sessions at which each of the main political parties was asked about their stance towards advertising and the industry.

Voting with my head rather than my heart, I chose the red corner, where Helen Goodman, MP for Bishop Auckland and Shadow Culture Minister, represented Labour in conversation with Jonathan Freedland of The Guardian and Robert Senior of Saatchi/Fallon.

Freedland's moderation was a bit quick for the audience because of his liberal use of double and triple negatives. This is probably a) because he's cleverer and quicker than the rest of us and b) because it's an age-old trick to catch an interviewee off guard.

But it was once Ms Hammond started that things took a turn for the worse. It became clear very quickly that she was neither well-briefed, nor in any way hospitable to industry's cause.

Gambling and HFSS foods were marched straight to the executioner's block. Nary a whiff of understanding about how important our industry is to business and the economy, nor of the difference between (entirely legal) products or services and their advertising. A high (by which I mean low) point was when it had to be pointed out to her that there were no ads in Eastenders. Oh dear.

This performance exacerbated the many extant concerns about the current Labour leader's attitude toward business. Fifteen months out from a general election and ahead of closer European elections that, like local elections, are set to hold little favour for the main parties in power, we had expected some form of charm offensive, however insincere.

Poor old Robert didn't get a word in. All the questions, challenges and widespread sighs – some of the most incredulous from self-declared labour supporters like Twitter's Bruce Daisley and party member Tess Alps of Thinkbox – were directed at the Honourable Member for Bishop Auckland.

By contrast, I gather that in the blue corner incumbent Culture Minister Ed Vaizey played his usual turn and enamoured himself to his assembled crowd.

This is not about (my) political preferences, though I unashamedly grant you that they may be clear. It's about how a party presents itself to a group of business voters – and it being our industry, a pretty influential one at that – in the run-up to what is expected to be a closely-fought battle with a highly uncertain outcome.

Unlike Labour to be so obviously asleep at the wheel; probably too busy currying votes in some provincial high street. I gather Conservative Central Office was also somewhat distracted, re-tweeting our disaffected tweets like crazy!

March 2014

When is clever too clever?

It seems everybody is talking about content marketing. It surfaces two big questions: what is it, and; how should it best be undertaken?

What is content marketing?

Short answer – how long is a piece of string?

But more seriously, it seems to be anything from old-fashioned advertorial, through to the creation and placement in the media of advertiser-created or funded audiovisual content on screens in or out of home, to pages and promoted comments in social media. And probably well beyond.

Thankfully, we have passed through the bullshit barrier wherein good 'advertorial' was renamed 'native marketing' by the digerati. With such a wide definition, it's not surprising that everybody's doing it. Or claiming to. And with 'supply' outstripping advertiser demand, the arguments about who is best qualified to deliver have started.

There is a lot of confusion, not least among clients, about who they should best use for what. This is not good as it leads to poor decisions and, in turn, bad work."

For instance, should media agencies have 'content divisions' and can we expect them to be any good at it? Can creative agencies used to TV making commercials write long-form or should it be left to experienced scriptwriters?

For what they're worth, my answers, respectively: sure, if they're any good at it, and time will tell, and; sometimes, and let's not forget that the agencies who did early TVCs best in the 50s and 60s poached theatrical and radio types to sit alongside their print-steeped creatives.

It's not at all clear to me that all this confusion is commercially justified. For example, my last column glanced on the changing economics of the creation of audiovisual content – the same piece of work can cost ten times as much if it is briefed as a TVC than if it is briefed as online video or viral. I'm often meeting with content creation companies who claim to be able make whole TV series for less than the price of a typical 30-second TVC nowadays.

What is clearer to me is that there is a lot of confusion, not least among clients, about who they should best use for what. This is not good as it leads to poor decisions and, in turn, bad work.

How should it best be undertaken?

This brings me to my main gist.

Most consumer research is feeding back the 'insight' that consumers are growing more savvy, a trend helped in no small part by widespread internet access. The newly-empowered consumer behaviour is demonstrated well by the middle classes, where savvy shoppers will make some of their purchases at Waitrose and some at Aldi, the supermarket as 'lifestyle badge' gradually giving way to 'repertoire shopping'.

The importance of openness and transparency to content marketing is as important as it is to the more serious issue of how online data is used."

For many years, people have been more and more able and inclined to read and decode advertising messages. There's a lot of evidence that many actually enjoy doing so.

However, we need to be careful. So many of our commercial communications techniques come from the US, but over there, consumers are used to and even like being sold to all of the time, whereas we Europeans (get me – all modern and federal) aren't and don't. This is especially so with us Brits.

Increasingly, international marketers and their partners talk about seamless interweaving of messages into content. Invisibility of any join is a source of pride.

But let's return to the newly-empowered, enlightened consumer on this side of the pond. They can see the join and, remember, they don't necessarily like it. Indeed, instead of being impressed by such 'cleverness', many react with hostility if they feel commercial intent is concealed rather than signalled and declared. Not so clever after all, then.

But there is a fine line to tread. We do, after all, react positively to openness, especially when the marketer has gone to considerable lengths to produce truly engaging content. In this context, my favourite user of content marketing, by a long chalk, is Red Bull.

Sure it uses spot advertising a bit, but pretty much anyone in its target market knows them best for literally owning F1 and extreme sports and all the amazing and engaging content these event-centric opportunities provide.

I'm not a great fan of the product myself, but talk about focus and consistency. And then, just when we thought they'd licked it, they stepped up a gear by literally going stratospheric with Felix Baumgartner jumping to Earth from space. Respect.

The importance of openness and transparency to content marketing is as important as it is to the more serious issue of how online data is used, too. But perhaps that's for another day.

April 2014

Can trading desks come 'clean'?

Bob Wootton raises some important questions on the nature of trading desks – and asks what it really means for an agency to be 'clean'.

A nasty virus may have meant my missing out on Ad Week, but at least I had London Live to keep me company last week.

Although I suspect I'm some way removed from its target market, I am impressed by what seems to be a single-minded pursuit of an aggressively-differentiated programme offering.

To its detractors I ask: that's got to be better than yet more of the same, surely?

But I digress; what I want to get my teeth into today is the concept of a 'clean' agency trading desk.

Almost a year ago I heard rumblings that a 'very big' trading group was looking to launch a 'clean' trading desk. Given that this was some months before the Publicis-Omnicom announcement, it was pretty safe to assume who the trading group in question was.

Recent chatter suggests that this launch will be soon, although not yet imminent, and could be followed by others. So, a good time to bring up some of the more fascinating questions it raises:

The trouble with absolute definitions is that one always defines the other"

– What is a 'clean' trading desk, and does this mean all others are 'dirty'?

– How clean is 'clean', anyway?

– And, most intriguingly, how does the owner of a 'clean' trading desk market it without critically undermining the incumbent?

These are questions that I have yet to see posed by others, let alone answered, and I am sure that my attempts to do so will not be met with universal accord. Actually, I would be fascinated by what others think...

Let's start with the binary definitions of 'clean' and 'dirty'. Given what a trading desk does – buy media, probably automatically and sometimes in real time, informed by rich data – the only variable that might lead to a desk being classified in such a way would be how transparent it is to clients, with those practicing arbitrage manifestly 'dirty'.

But the trouble with absolute definitions is that one always defines the other: if you aren't good you are bad; if you aren't right you are wrong; and so the emergence of a 'clean' trading desk effectively reclassifies (all) others as 'dirty'.

As it happens, the widespread industry view is that all trading desks operate arbitrage models. So, a 'clean' trading desk could make quite a splash among the larger and/or savvier clients who, while often paying low fees to these desks themselves, are not at all happy about covert profiteering on their accounts.

Doubtless there will be much wailing and gnashing of teeth here, and I'm not going to reheat some of the points I have made in a previous column relating to transparency. Suffice to say that with serious questions now being asked from many sides of the industry as to the margins being earned from complex media 'food chains' like digital, the announcement and arrival of a 'clean' trading desk will attract considerable attention.

If trading desks are going to purport to be 'clean' they are going to have to prove it"

Moreover, I gather that despite understandable pressure from their media agencies, who seek to consolidate their precious accounts, a number of major clients are declining to fold their businesses into agencies' trading desks, instead exploring independent, or even in-house, routes. Could this be the market force that's driving the new 'clean' product pitch from agencies?

But how clean is 'clean' anyway? Proponents in the space know just how devilishly difficult it is, even for dedicated specialists, to get under the bonnet of these things. Clients might believe complete transparency is not a deliverable proposition, and more a clever bit of market positioning. Frankly, if trading desks are going to purport to be 'clean' they are going to have to prove it.

But the question which promises the most mischief is, how does the owner of a 'clean' trading desk market it as such without critically undermining the incumbent?

Let's earwig an imagined lunchtime conversation, one which might be happening any day now. Nigel, marketing director of Scrumptious Foods Corp., is being entertained at L'Avenue by his media agency's group account director, Clarissa. The atmosphere over the table is redolent with a 2007 Etienne Sauzet Puligny Montrachet Les Combettes:

Nigel: So, Clarissa, how are things at my agency and its holding group colleagues?

Clarissa: Well, Nigel, I think it's safe to say that we're all breathing a well-deserved sigh of relief as we finally seem to be escaping recession and re-entering a period of growth. At both agency and holding group level, we showed positive turnover and margin growth, 'best in class', as far as we can tell. We've also been investing heavily in our insight team and that was one of the things I wanted to talk to you about.

Nigel: Great, tell me more?

Clarissa: Well, as you know, Torquil and our planning team have been leading a massive consumer study on media effectiveness attribution, which draws on our group's world-leading insight resources. The study has thrown up mountains of incredibly useful and sometimes surprising findings and the team is scheduling appointments to present the relevant outputs to each of our clients now.

At the risk of pre-empting the full two-hour PowerPoint, the long and the short for you is that we'll be recommending a significant shift of your budget from TV into 'online', going forwards.

Nigel: Gosh. That will be a big change – it's not so long ago that we reaffirmed our wedding vows with TV – in the face of significant pressure from out-of-home, as I recall!

Clarissa: You're right, Nigel. But our job is to embrace the latest and best insight we can and to help you adapt your marketing plans accordingly. And this comprehensive study points the way.

Nigel: OK, but there's another dimension here. We know what we're getting on the box, and we've spent a lot of time and money with you convincing ourselves that it's been working. Most of my peers operating in the online space talk about it like it's still bandit country; middlemen taking slices, concerns over brand-safe environments, more than half of ads not being viewed by real people, click fraud...

Clarissa: Well, pending the bigger media planning discussion and decision, at least I can set your mind straight there. You're right, it's been murky, but very shortly we'll be launching our new 'clean' trading desk, which should, at a stroke, allay many of these fears.

Nigel: That's really interesting. But as a brand guy, I have real trouble with that. What you're saying to all us clients, in effect, is that what you've been offering us hitherto is 'dirty', not transparent or compliant, but it's all going to be okay now with this new 'clean' thing. That's a pretty corrosive pitch, Clarissa. And how will you prove that 'new cleano' really does wash whiter?

Clarissa: Well, like I said re our future media plans for your brands, it's very early days as yet, Nigel. Very much embryonic and obviously subject to much fine-tuning by the powers-that-be, informed by conversations like this one. Tell me, where will you and family be holidaying this summer?

Nigel: Oh, probably a week windsurfing with the kids on Hayling Island or some such. You?

Clarissa: Sebastian and I have just booked a trip to Bora Bora. So romantic...

Ok, in my fevered state I may have incurred some penalty points on my dramatic licence to illustrate the situation, but wouldn't you just love to be a fly on the wall when the marketing of 'clean' trading desks starts...?

May 2014

Does the Pono bring an opportunity for premium streaming?

We've been short-changed by Apple and the MP3 revolution – but could the Pono offer a high quality alternative to iTunes?

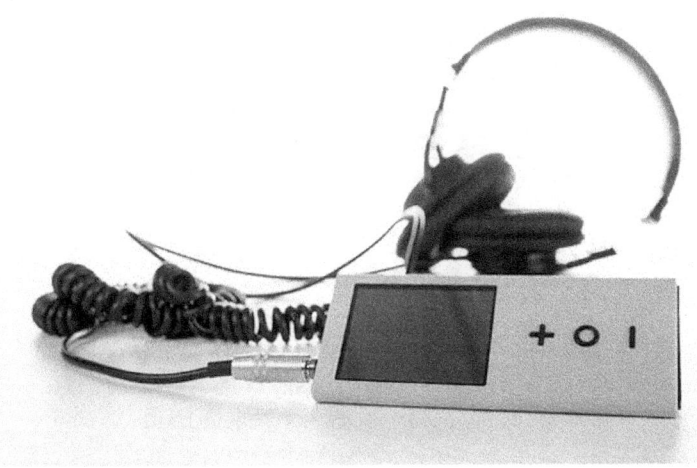

Given my double life – adman/lobbyist by day, musician by night – I spend a fair amount of time thinking about both music and the business of music as well as the business of media.

What prompted me was all the noise around the Kickstarter crowdfunded Pono device, backed by no less a name than Mr Crazy Horse himself, Neil Young.

Pono is a high-quality portable media player. The larger hi-res music files it stores and plays demand more storage, so the entry level player has a capacity of 128GB, several times that of your average smartphone and allegedly capable of storing about 2,000 songs. That's about what I have on my 16GB iPhone, which is enough to clog the memory and make software updates a real chore.

Storage being so compact these days, the Pono founders' choice of a triangular prism (Toblerone) shape is a rather curious design for something that could and should slip into a jean pocket.

As there's no market for hardware without content, Pono also promises an online store for hi-res digital music files like those which already change hands between hi-fi enthusiasts. A 'high-quality iTunes', if you like.

This is where my thinking turned grumpy, because I suddenly realised how short-changed we've been by Apple, a company whose products I otherwise tend to love. Let's look back...

Once there was vinyl (I'm discounting reel-to-reel tape, which was never a consumer phenomenon even in the days before such terms existed). With all its inconveniences – easily scratched, bulky, only played for 20 minutes before needing changing etc – carefully looked after, to the discerning music fan especially vinyl sounded really, really good.

Many years on, it still does. So much so that vinyl has defied its doomsayers and continues to make resurgences. It was always the choice of DJs for its tight, organic bass, and amongst enthusiasts for its warmth and finer detail across the spectrum. It's currently enjoying yet another modest boom amongst people who care about sound. (Costly tube/valve amplifier sales are also booming, but that's another, albeit connected, story).

Then we got compact cassette tapes. Very convenient – they worked in cars and some could run for longer than the twenty minutes of a vinyl LP.

But for manufacturing efficiency, they were recorded at high speed and because of their narrow tape being played back at low speed they were disappointingly lo-fi. Over time, they became the cheap, nasty alternative to vinyl, but still did big business for some years.

Pono makes me wonder if there isn't an incremental business opportunity here for Spotify – 'super-premium streaming' of the same high-quality audio files that Pono is punting."

Moving quickly past the dreadful and forgettable US-centric phenomenon of 8-track audiocassettes, we got to CDs. Launched by a dear mate of mine who came up with the (quite fraudulent) idea of smearing a disc with marmalade to demonstrate on live TV how resilient these things were, they raised the bar and offered great convenience and much higher-quality sound to many more people.

But to those that cared they still didn't sound as good as vinyl, a debate which rages even today, almost 40 years later.

Sidestepping the further flops of Mindisc (mini, enclosed CDs) and Digital Audio Tape (like mini VHS tapes, duh), along came the record-industry slayer, the digital music file format, and iTunes stepped into the breach to 'become' music retail. It has cornered the market with about two-thirds of all sales – a nice earner indeed. (Though for all their protestations of doom, the intermediated record companies' costs collapsed as they no longer had to manufacture the media on which their content is delivered).

History lesson over. My grump focuses on price versus quality, because MP3s and their like, whilst convenient as heck, don't sound so great. Better than cassettes, sure, but nowhere near CD-quality, let alone vinyl. Yet allowing for the gradual and long-term decline in pricing overall, their cost is comparable with the superior formats they have supplanted.

So net, and regardless of the consumer benefit of a more convenient way of searching for and buying albums and individual tracks, people are being sold an inferior-quality music format for at best a more or less parity price.

Regular readers will know that I love Spotify, but have long wondered about its business model and why it doesn't drop the price of Premium so it picks up many more paying subscribers. (I now understand that this is because they make more from advertising interventions to non-paying subscribers than they can from paying subscribers).

Nevertheless, the announcement of Pono makes me wonder if there isn't an incremental business opportunity here for Spotify – 'super-premium streaming' of the same high-quality audio files that Pono is punting. It looks technically possible as it's certainly not as bandwidth hungry as video streaming of almost any kind. And if Pono's backers are after a big 'push to market' this could be it.

Selfishly, I'd love to see consumer-friendly distribution of hi-res audio files beyond Pono devices alone. Indeed, I can imagine the re-emergence of a stratified market in which people acquire or access the music they love best on higher-priced hi-res formats, while they pay less for more disposable music on cheaper formats like MP3. (Just like we once did CD's, vinyl and cassettes).

Of course, over time, this will signal a reduction in the price of MP3s. But that would be nothing more than a market in operation, and what's wrong with that?

Transparency vs. independence?

Since my last column, **'Can Trading Desks Come Clean?'**, I've had a lot of incoming, which is great. It seems that many advertisers are quite rightly now asking questions that strike to the heart of the transparency of their trading desk arrangements.

The independent players are understandably jumping in with claims of greater transparency. I say 'claims' because firm proof is harder to come by and auditors are clearly playing catch-up in the online space.

Tom Denford of consultancy ID Comms has **published an interesting commentary on this dilemma recently**[iv]. I think we're going to hear a lot more noise, and then hopefully much greater clarity, in this important space. More anon, as they say...
R.I.P.P.O.G.

The courtship announced at a high-profile Parisian rooftop tryst last July is officially over. Decoy rumours over 'regulatory hurdles' and 'taxation issues' morphed into Thursday's announcement of the termination of the unconsummated merger between Publicis Groupe and Omnicom Group inc.

It's a victory for competition, but God only knows at what cost to the two parties. Estimates of £200 million are circulating, plus the damage to personal and corporate reputations and the legion human consequences. And naturally enough WPP's Sir Martin Sorrell is feasting on the outcome.

June 2014

Bonfire of the JICs?*

Forces are at play that could change the way we measure media – and Bob Wootton wonders if a more fragmented media audience could pave the way for more collaborative research.

One of the first industry events I attended after joining ISBA in April 1996 was Admap's 'Bonfire of the JICs' gathering.

To quote **Newsline's coverage of it at the time**[v], "Chaired by James Best, chairman of BMP DDB Needham and held at the Café Royal, the conference examined the theory that JICs could be done away with, or put on the 'bonfire', and that research could be carried out individually by separate media bodies."

James' illustrious career has continued – after chairing the Advertising Association, inter alia he now chairs CAP and BCAP, the bodies that determine what can and can't be said in ads.

As for the event itself, it was, unsurprisingly, inconclusive, though it did give vent to some strong views. It also gave me an early taste of something I would have to become used and inured to as the advertisers' representative, when a senior agency media director (now retired, but I'll spare his blushes anyway) told me in full session to "shut the fuck up and sit down". Happy days.

I represent advertisers on all the bodies that generate the UK's media research 'currencies': BARB, RAJAR, ABC, NRS, Route, UKOM and JICREG. And with that perspective, almost twenty years on, I smell woodsmoke.

How do I reach this conclusion? Well, as I look around I see common vectors and forces at work. The 'strong forces' first:

Advertisers are delegating and deferring more and more to their agencies. Few have a point of view or much engagement with the currencies that underpin their often considerable investments in media. And very few feel the need to subscribe directly to media research data any more.

Agencies are still pretty engaged and we should be very grateful for the many agency leaders who still involve themselves to ensure effective governance. Agencies also underwrite and/or part-fund the costs of a number of industry surveys. But at the same time agencies invest heavily, both in their own proprietary tools and in their industry body's (IPA's) ground-breaking cross-media TouchPoints survey, now on its fifth iteration.

That said, for their newer intakes, involvement in the currencies is not seen as interesting, nor career-critical. In some quarters, even a working knowledge is considered more or less unnecessary to one's ascent of the greasy pole.

Media Owners' relationship with the currencies remains as highly-charged as ever. A good quarter's results are trumpeted and monetised triumphantly; a bad quarter and it's all about the shortcomings of the research. They have the most money at direct risk and for that simple reason are also its major funders. But over recent years, the double whammy of recession and wholesale change across the media landscape has led to a significant funding shortfall.

Then there's the detail. The distribution of most media content is digital, leading to convergence in the measurability of each and all, and driving overlaps in the ambits of all the different legacy bodies.

BARB is by some way the best-funded of our industry currencies and has an aggressive plan to embrace hybrid methodologies to morph our nation's television viewing survey into a canvass of audiovisual media channels under a recently refreshed chair and CEO.

RAJAR is capable of embracing, and poised to embrace, measurement of streamed channels. However, its media owner stakeholders differ as to the desirability of this, which affects its scope and progress. Both BARB and RAJAR also count the 'non-commercial' BBC, an interesting and different influence, within their ranks.

The National Readership Survey has extended its canvass rather vigorously and effectively, cross-linking with inputs from UKOM to cover digital editions, although thus far sample sizes make this research more practical for the nationals than for most periodicals. But regardless of size, the question of saliency remains.

ABC is slightly different from all other JICs as it deals in audits of push-based metrics and not (panel-based) research. It has spent the past decade evolving from its legacy print-circulation audit base to embrace website pushes and has latterly become the industry's first port of call for evaluating and accrediting the many new and complex online metrics, again to widely varying degrees of enthusiasm from its media owner stakeholders.

JICREG models regional titles' audiences from ABC and publisher data, the pool of which is diminishing as that industry faces particularly lean times.

Route launched its new research into out-of-home in 2013 and continues to roll it out across all formats and estate. Like the industry sub-sector it serves, it can be a bit of a 'closed shop' with a tendency not to market what it has spent a decade and many millions developing, but the survey itself is undoubtedly a step-change and has considerable support and uptake from the specialist agencies.

UKOM is also something of an odd man out. Its governance is not strictly cross-industry and it doesn't oversee its own research survey but instead wrappers and steers a commercial offering – currently comScore. This is a (much) cheaper solution but one which affords less industry oversight.

Online media owners, especially the pure plays raised on analytics, have little time for the audience research that brands need and therefore have few qualms about spending less than any other channel on their audience research.

As audiences fragment and scatter across channels, it's getting more difficult to research them accurately. With difficulty comes added cost, but at a time when funding is less secure and more threatened.

The contractors capable of providing research to this market are relatively few, but on the positive side they continue to see UK industry contracts as a prize worth fighting for.

Joint industry bodies move slowly but, like democracy, are still the 'least worst' solution when compared with the alternative of media-owner owned or funded surveys skewed to producing bigger numbers.

True, they're reaching out to each other where there are glimpses of common cause, but given the pressures, how long can the multiple silo'ed bodies driven by the legacy agendas of their various media owner stakeholders persist?

It would be rash to call 1996's 'Bonfire Of The JICs' event prescient. Equally, the 'separate media bodies' thing would be a red herring but, notwithstanding turkeys and Christmas, maybe it's time to revisit a more streamlined, efficient, effective and collaborative future, lest Kantar's TGI simply sweeps the board.

Cannes of sour grapes?

It might just be me catching up late with a phenomenon that's been building for several years – and no, I wasn't there – but this year was the first year social media and the Cannes Festival really converged for me.

Maybe it's the company I keep, but my Facebook timeline was full of posts of our industry's leaders – sorry to say this, but mainly the laydeez – hanging out with slebs or each other at the rolling parties on or near beaches, now more or less taken over by the tech players.

Nice work if you can get it, but where were all the selfies with the Global CMOs that everybody says they're going there to meet? Nothing wrong with mixing business with pleasure, but broadcasting thus perhaps betrays a slight lack of judgement and self-awareness.

Unsung on the FB and Twitter feeds, there's an amazing amount of serious work done by the judges who wade through thousands and thousands of entries, locked away in darkened rooms away from la plage, La Croisette and the otherwise undrinkable Domaine D'Ott that substitutes for the water supply there.

Which makes it even more of a shame that it comes across more than ever as one humongous jolly to those of us who weren't fortunate enough to attend. Did I mention I wasn't there? Grrr.

*Joint Industry Committees

July 2014

Could dropping the National Readership Survey lose newsbrands money?

There's no apparent regard for the fact that a number of industry sources, including TGI, UKOM and RAJAR, are calibrated against the NRS population survey. If we kill the NRS much could fall apart.

'Press' readership research

However much I try to avoid the obvious trap of talking about media research, given my participation in the managements of all of the industry's currencies, sometimes it's unavoidable.

Indeed, I broke my own code of omerta in my last column, 'Bonfire of the JICs?' which yielded a rich postbag and presaged subsequent research-related events by just a few days.

I'm referring of course to the Newspaper Publishers Association's recent decision to initiate its own review into the future of 'readership' research.

Thinkbox's Tess Alps, always good for a considered and independent perspective, picked up on this and a couple of other serious industry issues in her blog[vi] for Brand Republic on July 18.

The newspapers, understandably buoyed by their success in reaching an unprecedented consensus on the specification of a new universal trading system – which they also hope to sell to periodicals – took a necessary step in disrupting the National Readership Survey (NRS) by serving it notice.

This certainly got their fellow stakeholders' attention. I'm on record for my view that they then overshot by taking the further and unwarranted step of announcing and initiating their own review and effectively signalling UDI.

This puts them at odds (albeit rather different odds) with each of their fellow industry stakeholders and wounds NRS – whose new CEO has been in place for a mere month, incidentally – grievously if not yet fatally.

There's also no apparent regard for the fact that a number of other industry sources, including TGI, UKOM, RAJAR and JICREG, are calibrated against the NRS population survey. No NRS, no calibration and much could fall apart, or at least cost everybody, including newsbrands, a lot more money.

Having been a director of NRS for nearly twenty years, I could mention that for many of those it was the newspapers' representatives on a then-bloated board who most often deadballed any attempts to drive progress.

And from a number of conversations with some of their leading lights, I could also confirm their mounting frustrations with audience research as circulations and readerships declined and revenues become more challenging.

But clear as I am on the depth of their frustrations I am equally unclear as to what they actually want, though the words 'responsiveness' and 'engagement' come up most frequently.

True, joint industry governance is slower-moving than unilaterally-commissioned research. Forging a consensus between media-owner desire for big numbers (more revenue) and advertisers' search for something approaching a credible 'truth' takes time.

The NRS has also been dogged by the natural tension between newspapers (latterly 'newsbrands') and magazines (or whatever they're going to call themselves in future). On the plus side, the more funders for the survey, the broader the base across which its significant costs are amortised.

The presence of 'mags' also drives accuracy, as many of their titles' smaller readerships are harder to measure and force a larger sample. But then the two camps compete for some of their revenue and sell differently, albeit to an overlapping group of agency and advertiser buyers.

'Responsiveness' includes frequency of publication, the argument being that quarterly is insufficient for titles that appear (at least) daily. By contrast BARB measures and reports TV viewing continuously, but before we get too carried away, let's remember that its constituents also sink over £25m into it each year, compared to NRS' (approximate) £4m.

Moreover, BARB's diverse constituents are sensible and mature enough to see the merits to progress of inclusive collaboration for a greater good, and its (newish) leadership are up for it, embracing and driving change.

'Responsiveness' also wrappers publishers' age-old gripe that circulation and audience can move in opposite directions, often publicly-laundered in their people's individual sales meetings. While one might expect these data to track each other, it is still possible for one to move one way and one the other, especially when the differences in the capture mechanisms – ABC audit vs NRS panel research – are considered.

'Engagement' is about the depth of relationship with the reader. The more this can be claimed and proven, the better the price that can arguably be obtained for media space. It's also something of a holy grail for agencies and media owners alike, all of whom would love to proffer better metrics to advertiser customers eager for such insight.

Perversely, the dear old NRS (around since 1954) contains several useful quantitative indicators of 'engagement': time spent reading, proportion of title viewed. And as it has striven to extend to cover tablet and mobile editions (subject to the readerships being big enough to research), it has captured more relevant data.

The 'engagement' that NPA's members are seeking must therefore be something else/more than what they're already paying for and have to hand.

Anyway, we must look forward positively to finding out what the NPA's members want and engaging hopefully and optimistically for a good outcome. There's a lot riding on this for the newsbrands – their ad revenues, to be precise – so it had better be good. Advertisers have some choice as to where to put their ad budgets these days.

The toxic cesspit (continued)

In his July 21 piece, my fellow **contributor Dominic Mills raked over the emerging mess that is the online display market under this title**[vii].

Sadly, much of what's emerging makes grim reading. It's been claimed that less than 50% of ad budgets actually appear as 'working media' (the term many major advertisers use to describe an opportunity for their target consumers to see their marketing comms and that has had to be coined simply because so much of their money is siphoned off in fees and other 'costs').

Then we hear that less than 50% of these 'impressions' are viewable by humans.

These assertions have been unchallenged for months now, which gives them validity, and they're averages, so some will be doing better and some worse. This means that we can commute the two figures, which means that some 75% of online display adspend is at best misplaced, and worse, wasted. Now that is a scandal.

Even with the protection of the City of London Police Intellectual Property Crime Unit (PIPCU)'s Infringing Website List and the joint industry-agreed Good Practice Principles to help protect brands – both worthy but a long time coming – there is also the continuing issue of reputable, responsible advertisers' brand ads appearing in some very, very unsavoury places.

Since a high and growing proportion of online inventory is traded impression by impression in real time, there are billions, if not trillions, of ad trades. So it's easy to see how a few can slip through, particularly when unscrupulous networks or aggregators are involved and feasting on the attendant revenues.

And now the **FT confirms that things are yet worse**[viii]. Attribution of advertising effect is still usually ascribed to the last click, not because it's right, but because despite 'big data' it's still difficult to unpick consumers' journeys and attach value to each step of their way. The crims have clocked this and figured how to create lots of fraudulent click traffic, distorting real reads of effect and diverting booming ad budgets into dark places.

Nobody seems that fussed about cleaning things up, but perhaps this is not so strange. I'd venture two reasons: tons of money is being made regardless, and the earnout horizons in the space are much shorter.

So there's a major opportunity – not to say a solemn responsibility – for the same IAB that has been such a great flag-bearer for the media it represents to step in and take a much more robust leadership stance amongst its members, however uncomfortable, before the bad reputation sticks and worried money migrates.

And while on this topic, you really should read **this blog**[ix] entry. It may not be in the language and tone that is expected of me, but I found myself smiling and agreeing wholeheartedly with its content and sentiments.

That damn BARB

Respected media veteran Tim Kirkman, now a senior executive at ESI, has lashed out at BARB as an exclusive club for the big broadcasters following its reports of depressed ratings for its London Live channel.

Before one even gets into who BARB's controlling stakeholders are, there are good technical and financial reasons why panel research favours the bigger players whose media have bigger audiences (see 'Press Readership Research' above).

But rather than bemoan the status quo loudly, ESI might better put its money where its mouth is and fund a boost to BARB's London panel so it can test and perhaps prove its point.
Like community radio, local television is a result of a political vision – hence its preferential positions on the various electronic programme guides – and not market demand from consumers or advertisers.

And it's a competitive space. Although regional opt-outs are scarcer on ITV and Channel 4 these days, Sky's Adsmart allows regional, even local, targeting within some very good broadcast content indeed.

Happy holidays, all.

September 2014

I'll pay you (much) later

Any agency that is asked to accept greatly delayed payment terms is effectively being asked to bankroll its client. Is this a growing trend we should be worried about?

Having been away from the office for more than half the time since my last column (very nice break, thanks, since you ask) I'm still perhaps a little demob happy. Perhaps that explains my recklessly opining on a(nother) very controversial subject – extended payment terms.

I should say first of all that the views I express are entirely my own, but are obviously informed by my near 40-years' experience in industry.

Over the past couple of years, some large companies have reportedly sought to improve their cash flow and treasury income by imposing greatly extended payment terms on their suppliers. In the ad game, where huge sums of advertisers' money destined for the media channels pass through agencies, this has understandably led to some grave concerns.

Most of the money that goes to agencies goes on the media costs themselves, with the smaller part providing the fees from which they pay operating costs and make profits. Agencies which can satisfy the media of their creditworthiness and good financial standing get 'recognised' which means they can buy media on credit and not have to pay for it in advance.

Each of the media channels has its own payment terms, but very broadly the standard terms require payment for TV spots 15 days after the month in which they appeared, and for other media it's 30 days.

Now these are of course the standard terms. Today's consolidated mega media buyers are masters of trade and money and have legion terms of their own like AVBs, payment extension, or this year's newbie, 'services'. None of which are understood to be nearly as long as the extensions prompting this discussion.

It is of course up to any supplier to decide whether they are happy to have their own incomes deferred for the sake of continued trade, but they can't be nearly as flexible on the (much larger) payments due to their suppliers unless they can pass the pain down the value chain. So any agency that is asked to accept greatly delayed payment terms is effectively being asked to bankroll its client.

Now if I wanted to borrow money, I'd go to a bank. Hopelessly naïve, you might say, but I thought media agencies planned and bought media. So I would find it quite understandable if an agency either demurred to a client's request demand to pay late.

Or if they were to agree, it would be on the understanding that they could charge the interest they would incur from their own bankers plus an admin fee for being and doing something they aren't and don't.

I realise these diktats often originate from a centralised finance function perhaps thousands of miles away – often in the land where the biggest money talks loudest and pushes hardest – and that different countries have different business customs and practices, but I can't help question both the underpinning morality and wisdom.

Consider the employee relationship and CSR dimensions. Are rank and file employees proud to work for companies that don't pay for what they consume for months? And how do customers feel? The notion of corporate bullying surfaces pretty quickly, especially when you consider the way social media amplify and accelerate conversations today.

Word has it that the imminent party conference season will see some renewed pushes against lengthy payment terms. Government has already announced new legislation to be introduced later this year that will require public sector organisations to pass 30 day payment terms down through their supply chains.

It also proposes to work with industry bodies and business stake holders to promote sector based best practice approaches and promises better enforcement of current penalties for late payment.

Business Secretary, Vince Cable, said: "For too long too many large companies have been getting away with not paying their suppliers on time to maximise their profits. It is small businesses that are suffering as a result and it needs to stop.

"The government has taken action to create a responsible payment culture but we need to go further. We will now make it compulsory for large companies to publish information about their payment practices so that those who are not playing fair can be held to account."

They say charity begins at home, so I thought I might contact my bank, energy, satellite TV and broadband suppliers and the retailers I use off and online and tell them that henceforth I'll be paying my bills six months hence. What kind of response do you think I'll get?

Whither broadcast major sporting events?

I don't follow much sport myself, but even for a Philistine like me the migration of the UEFA Champions League to BT Sport from ITV (and Sky) raises some interesting issues as we enter the annual trading round bun-fight.

It highlights obvious differences in business models – ITV unwilling to pay more for rights than it can earn from the advertising within its coverage and Sky from its subscribers vs. BT loss-leading on to drive more profitable and core broadband penetration.

But BT Sport's penetration is a fraction of ITV's universal footprint, so with the best will in the world the events it carries will achieve much smaller audiences.

This is bad in the short term for the advertisers who use these events to reach their audiences in large numbers. And bad for ITV – I've heard more than one major advertiser aver that they're "really only on ITV for the sport", so if the sport offer diminishes (and they have also lost the FA Cup rights to the BBC for four years too), so could their spend.

You can't blame the rights holders, in this case UEFA, for maximising revenue in the short term, but in the longer term I see it as bad news for them too as major events' franchises and value dwindle without mass coverage. Right now, it's a war of attrition between free-to-air and the pay platforms.

As for the football fans? Well they now have to contemplate multiple pay platforms to see what they used to get in return for the licence fee and/or having to tolerate some world-class ads.

Granted, the final is on the protected list of events which must be free to air, but I wonder how long it will be before the Commons Culture, Media & Sport Select Committee's energetic chairman John Whittingdale MP decides to seize on this?

This week in Scotland

This Thursday sees the Scots going to the ballot box to decide if they want to remain a part of the UK. I personally think voting 'Yes' would not be beneficial to their economy or our combined standing in the world, but polling suggests it will be very close.

Westminster has been rattled enough by the polls to give (too) many concessions if the Union remains in place, but the likely margin either way could be so slim that we should expect whoever is in opposition to claim that the winner hardly has any mandate to govern.

Closer to home, Nigel Walley of Decipher has written a characteristically excellent blog piece on the implications of a 'Yes' vote for the broadcasting industry both sides of the border which you can find **here**[x].

And given the national frenzy up there, I wonder what ratings the coverage on the night will achieve?

October 2014

Building brands with one hand; killing them with the other?

Companies spend millions building and protecting their brands, but then ruin it all with terrible customer service.

The Institute of Practitioners in Advertising recently published a study, by the godfathers of effectiveness, Les Binet and Peter Field, called 'The Long and the Short Of It'. It's an excellent and definitive examination of the past thirty-two years of the IPA Advertising Effectiveness Awards to determine the effects of long and short-term advertising strategies.

One of its key conclusions is that brands deliver greater and more sustainable profit than mere products. So brands are profitable, but they're delicate too.

I was at a dinner recently when the customer interface became the subject of discussion, and that debate really got me thinking.

In my world, companies spend millions on building and protecting their brands, and I spend my working life doing my best to protect their interests.

So why would many of those selfsame brand owners embark on parallel activities which are damaging, corrosive even, to their delicate, hard-earned brands?

Ask anybody you know and they will surely have a ready story about a 'customer experience' with a customer help line or call centre.

Whether the recounted 'experience' starts with a harmless customer query or a complaint, say about service delivery, the tale will invariably involve frustration, escalation and ultimately dissatisfaction with how they were handled.

Customer service is big business both globally and in the UK. According to Cognito, in 2013 there were 5,675 call centres in the UK employing 1,125,000 people. That means nearly 4% of the UK workforce are employed in this part of the industry.

Many of the large businesses which effectively make up the fabric of consumer society – utilities, retailers, banks and so on – obviously need to have ways of dealing with their customers. No issue there.

And there are millions and millions of them, so these systems need to be capable of sometimes handling very high traffic, particularly at times of stress or crisis.

Moreover, although there will be commonality – (most) people don't phone their bank to grumble about their gas supply, for example – each contact is likely to be somewhat different, so the systems have to be flexible and capable of directing customers quickly and efficiently to the right people.

Ok, that's the spec written and it wasn't too hard, was it? But what about the delivery?

Back to those large businesses that make up the fabric of consumer society. All claim to be customer-facing these days because that's the right thing to say. The mantra of "we really value each and every opportunity to engage with our customers" usually surfaces in the same breath.

Fair enough, but why then do so many make such a hash of it?

– Automated option-based telephone systems, several/many minutes' waiting time, few or no options for callbacks

– Call centres, often offshored, populated by people with insufficient grasp of the customers' local geographies or customs, and often language – but usually with plenty of time on their hands

– The requirement to provide personal information before being allowed to proceed which customers would rightly expect to be passed and put on operators' screens as the call is progressively channelled towards the right customer service operative

– All this going on while the customer is pressed for time because they're probably making calls from their workplace or in a break during office hours.

Remember, these are invariably either new or existing customers, not strangers. Yet many companies have seen commercial opportunity and turned their customer operations into businesses, charging at premium rates and keeping people waiting.

Most phones show call duration nowadays, so it's easy to see how long you've been kept waiting and figure out the cost.

And now, there's the rush for data that can be used for marketing and retargeting, or brand stalking as some prefer to see it nowadays.

Some frankly terrifying stats to confirm what you're fearing. The average Brit:

– spends up to 27 minutes waiting each time they phone a call centre. This accrues to 22 days over a lifetime

– wastes up to £385 a year – or £30,780 over an average lifetime – paying for time spent waiting when phoning call centres, according to a new national survey. (Sources : OnePoll, 2013)

– spend up to 6 ½ hours a year waiting on the line when phoning call centres. The summary of this poll comments that, "This significant length of time could have otherwise been spent flying to New York, running a marathon or watching the original Star Wars trilogy."

– 66% of UK consumers polled in 2012 believed that customer service had either stayed the same or deteriorated over the past three years. Only 3% thought it had improved a lot and 22% a little. (Sources: Cognito)

Look here[xi] if you want to see some major UK utilities' performance. It's grim.

I was in The Drewe Arms in Drewsteignton, north Dartmoor, with an old client, now a friend, the other day. The landlord was holding for his telephony provider's customer service line on his mobile whilst serving his admittedly few customers as the landline was down and he was losing meal reservations.

Given that I was writing this piece, I asked him how long he'd been waiting – "43 minutes and counting and I'm quite used to it" was the reply. Only one instance, but as I say, everybody seems to have many more than one.

This has led to an evolution in customer behaviour.

Most people have figured out what strategies work and get you connected quickly. With utilities including mobile telephony, you either dial the sales number (they answer that line very quickly!) or better, follow the channel for cancelling your contract (which is populated by operatives who are empowered to help and not just suck your time).

Better still is to do away with calls to a customer line altogether and go straight to Twitter. That gets a really rapid response, as companies are clearly and rightly very concerned about their reputation and do not want customers bad-mouthing their brands, products and/or services being dragged through the mud in full public view.

If you're not doing these things already, I recommend them.

What beats me is why so many companies continue to invest in but not improve systems that are so patently destructive to their brands' standing. It's universally-agreed that word of mouth is the most powerful marketing channel of all, so why would you invest in something so corrosive?

It's one thing for the likes of HMRC – 'services' that are unlikely to have many fans regardless and may therefore albeit misguidedly conclude that they have no need for any customer ethic whatsoever – but it's another entirely for any company that practices, let alone claims it understands, marketing.

November 2014

The Internet of Stupid Things

Just because we can put advertising everywhere doesn't mean that we should.

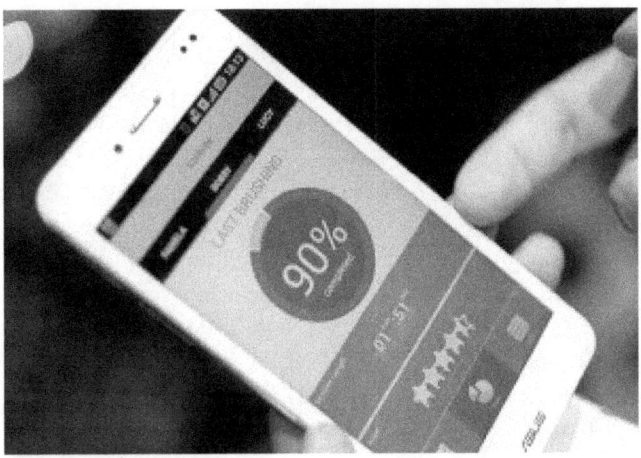

I'm indebted to David Rowan, editor of the UK edition of tech bible and coffee-table buster Wired, especially as the publication is quite often the cheerleader for some undoubtedly glamorous but sometimes rather questionable new tech.

But he's called it out right this time for me. All this talk of an 'Internet of Things' should be carefully filtered with the residues going to his aptly-named 'Internet of Stupid Things'.

He's outed some truly amazingly-stupid kitchen devices now coming to market, where else but the US. A bluetooth-equipped set of kitchen scales earnestly offers 'real-time insight to your food'. Like, er, how much each ingredient weighs. Cor. Cool. Nah.

We've all been nodding sagely to each other for years in the bars of E1 when someone posits the self-refilling fridge (which has yet to emerge anywhere outside an oligarch's duplex for obvious reasons).

Of course, it will as ever be 'all about data', but here too we should beware the siren voices of the pedlars."

And we've now seen the arrival to the mass-market of useful offerings like Nest and Hive, both promising remotely-addressable domestic protection (smoke and CO detection) and central heating control which could save us decent money and reduce our energy consumption footprint.

Yet sad as I usually am, I remain deeply unenthusiastic about communicating with my kettle, even if it's to ask it to boil water for my morning cuppa while I'm still upstairs brushing my teeth – with my toothbrush, which is at that very moment deluging my dentist with unwelcome details of how I am brushing and the state of my oral cavity. While my SmartCuff is informing my GP about my heart trace and my smart loo is deluging her with (analytics of) my morning constitutional. Enough of that. And like she will have time to care under the ongoing cuts anyway...

I would sometimes find it quite useful to be able to turn my oven on to heat my dinner when I'm on my way home. But then again, given all the legislation and regulations that clearly reveal how very stupid most of us are or are considered to be by those who govern us, those same people might think it quite dangerous to allow the remote control of devices that might boil, dry or otherwise overheat and set things on fire.

And as for running a bath remotely, I doubt home insurers are going to rush for that one. Now an app that put my bins out – not just a reminder – would be seriously useful, but I'm not holding my breath for that either.

All this gets me thinking about our tendency to try and put advertising everywhere, and how that might manifest itself in an Internet of Things, stupid or otherwise.

I can see a dishwasher with a screen interface and the ability to notify and perhaps even place an order when rinse aid or salt is low, and it would not be much of a leap to imagine ads for dishwasher tablets on that same screen. Similarly a washing machine.

Maybe the screen on my lawnmower (?!) will be able to tell me that I need to empty the grass box while I'm so busy watching it that I run over my foot and sever three toes. Clearly I need this, as just looking at an overflow of cuttings would not send me the same signals at all.

Doubtless there will be the usual headlong rush of enthusiasm for the new and media stunts galore as all this claptrap comes along."

But can I imagine with enthusiasm the new John Lewis ad running on these things? The good advice of 'make once, use many times' is all very well, but just because a piece of AV content can be screened on a device, does it follow that it should? How would it look and come across? Would it do the production justice or just be yet another 'because it's there' outlet?

Of course, it will as ever be 'all about data', but here too we should beware the siren voices of the pedlars. Advertising is a cardinal paymaster of a data industry that is showing some signs of being out of control. The press are now beginning to point this out and the regulators are noticing. We need to watch ourselves on this one.

Doubtless there will be the usual headlong rush of enthusiasm for the new and media stunts galore as all this claptrap comes along, but might we perhaps not do better first to sit back and take a rather more level view of how we wish the ads we place to be consumed?

Let's play tag: tackling online fraud

As I write, news reaches us from the US of an industry initiative to begin to tackle the very serious issue of online fraud.

The independent 'Trustworthy Accountability Group' (TAG) is being formed by three industry bodies – The Association of National Advertisers; the American Association of Advertising Agencies; and the Interactive Advertising Bureau. It will be led by Linda Woolley, a former CEO of the Direct Marketing Association.

Not a moment too soon, and I now gather that we too will be getting something similar off the ground here imminently.

I should say, though, that I'll be pressing for some outputs that are much more convincing than those of another US joint-industry endeavour. The Media Rating Council's recent definition of viewability – half the pixels in view for one second for static ads and for two seconds for video – falls so far below what we expect of linear TV as to be virtually (sic) meaningless.

December 2014

Ho, ho, ho, Bah humbug and some home truths?

Hello, all. Despite my occasional misdemeanours/outpourings they're still allowing me to contribute, so, in time-honoured fashion, as the year closes I'm going to join the many seasonal cliché-mongers and offer some thoughts and, dare I say, hopes for the year ahead.

I agree wholeheartedly that we're living through a time of unprecedented change, much of it brought on by the disruptive power of digital communications. But I also think that we remain a conservative business that often seeks to play down the very same disruptive forces that are bandied about in client presentations about pretty much anything.

The role of agencies is therefore changing and will continue to change. Having lost pretty much all the means by which they can make serious money (e.g. media, production decoupling) and under relentless client procurement pressure, creative agencies have tended towards man-hours and materials businesses. Not a lot of obvious margin growth opportunity there.

Yet content is superabundant, as everybody is posting everything. So with all the issues surrounding attention and engagement, or the lack thereof, there has never been such an important role for the professional creators and curators of high-quality content.

This means there are huge opportunities for creative agencies that produce really great, high-quality, well-finished work rooted in real consumer insight. Unfortunately, there are more agencies than work of this kind to go round and latterly there have even been reports of advertisers inviting media agencies to pitch against creative agencies for their creative accounts, some within the same holding group. Where on earth is that going?

What is quite clear is that media agencies are sharp, highly-adaptable businesses whose models have evolved far beyond many of their clients' imaginations and awareness, especially in the digital value chain. (I know, it's a shit term but nobody has come up with a better one yet so we have to live with it.)

Margins in 'digital' are an order of magnitude greater than in legacy media channels, delivered through multiple intermediaries, many commonly and or/mutually-owned. And all this has arisen without the advertiser clients' permission and has now reached worrying scale.

So to paraphrase The Killers, the big question every advertiser should ask their media agency in 2015 is 'are you agency or are you reseller?'

This is not about the smokescreen of financial principality, but about definitions. In the language of our industry, I venture that an agent works for and is funded by its clients, whereas a reseller trades in things it has committed to (i.e. aggregated volume commitments) and/or bought (i.e. arbitrage).

How can an agency that trades in bulk and/or commits to buys in advance offer its clients the channel-neutral counsel they should rightly seek? It can't, because it's already committed, or as we have seen this year, sometimes dangerously overcommitted.

While I'm here, we've seen some cracking use of English this year, with the subdivision of the word transparency! It is used simply to mean (advertisers') visibility of the financial undercurrents which drive their agencies' media selection and deployment.

But now we have 'transparent but undisclosed', which seems to mean 'you can look so far but no further'. Doubtless we'll see yet more semantic cleverness in this space in the future.

Recent initiatives emanating from the agencies' body, the IPA, which aim to reclaim the ear of the most senior client executives across disciplines – 'Adapt' and latterly 'Know The Value of Media' are strategically and narratively spot on. But I feel that they will founder while the messengers continue to appear to have their hands in the tills.

A more welcome development is the translation of transparency into the consumer space, as in "Is it clear that this is a commercial communication I'm seeing?" This is a welcome development – surely no reputable advertiser should be trying to gull a viewer surreptitiously?

Likewise, there's now much more airtime and space to fill than there is high-quality content, so while the future remains uncertain for the also-rans, a great opportunity remains for premium publishers and broadcasters.

Yet quite a few media owners, even big and powerful ones, are privately expressing concerns about how far things have gone, and how agency group business models have come to favour digital channels beyond the value they have yet to prove.

Talking of which, the industry needs to do lots more work to correlate and calibrate premium advertising inventory against the metrics of engagement, viewability, brand safety – and now fraud.

It would be great – not to say just – if premium, professionally-curated inventory could be convincingly shown to be both safer and more effective for brands. Critically this analysis should include all inventory, including the stuff that is arbitraged by some agency groups.

Such information should be rigorously conducted by the industry-verified content verification providers (five so far) and hopefully orchestrated and published under the aegis of the Internet Advertising Bureau. It could also give the lie to whether it is indeed right to **point the finger at procurement pressure**[xii] as the reason for excessive use of non-premium online inventory through aggregators, exchanges and blind buys, whether real-time or not.

Finally, we're seeing some serious challenges to the objectivity of the metrics on which trade is based. National newspapers' withdrawal from the National Readership Survey and subsequent tender for a new survey suggests change is likely and – hopefully – positive. Web standards are diverging from circulation metrics at ABC, which is probably overdue and a good thing. A challenge to the objectivity of a key input in out-of-home research has passed – for now.

Online audience research remains somewhat stunted by underfunding and mobile, tablet and multiplatform measurement, as well as the aforementioned viewability and non-human traffic all continue to present big challenges. Thank goodness, then, for stability and orderly progress at BARB and RAJAR which serve TV and radio respectively.

Back to my opening premise, change may be good but you can also have too much of a good thing.

And to round off 2014, if anyone is planning on taking themselves too seriously over the Christmas period, **here's a great online resource**[xiii].

Happy holidays and a preposterous 2015 to you all.

February 2015

Have we got the right trading system for today's market?

With resurgent volatility, are medialand's trading systems are sufficiently agile to cope?

The past few years, from before and right through the worst recession in memory, have seen many media prices static, if not declining in real terms.

Media, especially television, has not been the major cost input with unpredictable price and sometimes runaway cost for advertisers. Rather, they have enjoyed almost constant pricing arising from the economic climate and market innovation. Media cost inflation has not been a discussion point.

But buying reviews and audits of H1 2014 media activity last autumn saw recriminations as the market came back in a big way and prices surged well ahead of expectation in some months.

And so far this January, it looks like everybody's got it quite seriously wrong again. Costs are up about 20% (only yesterday somebody punted me 25%!) against an expected 7-8%. Oops. To paraphrase Oscar Wilde, "once is unfortunate, but twice is carelessness".

Advertiser demand is well ahead of expectation and a major driver – retail is up 25%, financials 20% and telecoms 19%. At the macro level, we should celebrate this because advertising has been shown to be a good and true bellwether of the broader economy.

And improving revenues make the position less precarious than it has been for some media, restoring profitability and making the generation of quality content more sustainable...

...provided that revenues continue to be reinvested in content and effective distribution, of course.

But unfortunately audiences are down too, creating compound inflation. Many advertisers are missing their targets or reluctantly having to inject more money to reach them, which only makes matters worse as it raises the market's rising price further. A rising tide lifts all boats.

This is leading to the rebirth of advertiser concerns about effective media owner investment in their product. And the word is that broadcasters are overtrading too – granted, there are 11 months left in which to reconcile annual deal books, but this is cold comfort for the brands whose time is now.

And stop press – just in, news of a letter from Five to its advertiser clients represented by Omnicom agencies questioning the wisdom of their non-use of the channel when it can claim its prices are lower and deflating unlike their competitors'.

All this raises two big questions:

1. Why can't we gauge the market better? and
2. Is the trading system still fit for purpose?

On gauging the market, it's self-evident that the bigger the media agency, the better its visibility of the market. Advertisers and media owners have precise knowledge of their own spends and takes respectively, but the bigger the agency, the broader view it will have and market consolidation means most are big enough.

During the recession, broadcasters sometimes flexed their advance booking deadlines, but as the market has returned, so these have once again stiffened so late money held back shouldn't explain things, at least not fully.

Yet the disappointment of shortfalls doesn't materially affect agencies like it does their clients' unless their remuneration is somehow geared in part to the accuracy of their forecasts (now there's a good idea for the next major advertiser pitching their media account...).

As for the trading system, most of the money is now tied up in big agency deals. If you believe some insiders, this even includes some of the agencies that profess not to operate agency deals. It's hard for advertisers to tell quite what's what these days.

These deals are big, can be complicated, doubtless all promise keen pricing, privileged programme access, bells and whistles etc, but now there's the question of whether they're sufficiently agile to cope with resurgent volatility. Indeed, it's been argued that the way major media are traded annually has become quite 'comfortable'. Just look at the key players' golf handicaps.

So how does an advertiser retain flex, whether to make its targets when it needs to, or simply to express its displeasure and swing its weight by rewarding strong performance and punishing failure if a particular media owner is not delivering?

Bound up in deal frameworks, this appears to be difficult for many. Once it was only ITV and C4 that mattered to reach, now every major player has a story and contribution to make. Volume and diversity should mean plenty of competition for ad budgets. Yet the positive incentive to perform and disincentive to fail are dulled – a perverse impact of agency deals.

Good news for advertiser opportunity and broadcaster revenues that the market is diversifying away from spot. But – pace Thinkbox, who will as ever jump on this of course – what if the reported structural changes in US TV viewing are now coming here? At least one of our leading members now looks there for an idea of how things are going to be here in a couple of years.

If there is indeed a trend towards other ways of watching 'telly' – which everybody still seems to love even they also deny they're doing it! – then advertisers will surely look to other audiovisual channels to make up the reach deficits. (As ever, frequency is relatively abundant and cheaper to chase.)

But advertisers are in the main pretty rigorous, and need data upon which to base such budget migration decisions which is – for the moment – rather lacking. Nielsen OCR helps, but has its supporters and detractors and is not an industry standard. And Nielsen's loss of the UKOM contract a couple of years back doesn't exactly help.

BARB is to be admired for working furiously to a stretching timetable to deliver its Project Dovetail, which will embrace all forms of viewing and promises advertisers what they seek, but it's not due until the end of the year (assuming all goes well) and advertisers are calling for information now.

This autumn's trading round ought to be the most interesting for years – but will old habits and massive group/bundled deals which largely favour the comfortable status quo and arguably hobble advertiser agility still prevail?

Vegas – a dry old place for damp squibs?

So another year and another Consumer Electronics Show has come and gone in Vegas. We keep a close eye on it in case anything comes to light that signals opportunity for marketers.

But despite delegates' evangelical belief that absolutely nothing shown there each year has ever been seen anywhere before, nothing much came out of this year's shindig (unless you're into internet-connected plant waterers).

To be fair, the gamification of children's toothbrushing was interesting and societally on-message and the ring that turns your hand into a (computer!) mouse would have been interesting were it not for the pre-existing motion sensing tech in our smartphones, tellies and game consoles which er, turns your whole body into a control surface. Ho hum.

March 2015

Is the game up for media auditing?

Auditing might still have a place in the UK media sector, but it's not set for growth.

I was around when the idea of media auditing – as in getting and pooling advertisers' bought TV costs and assessing their relative performance against the pool – was first conceived. By which, I mean I was in the office next door.

The world's first media auditing company was Media Audits, now found deep within Accenture. There was only one commercial TV channel back then, but it was sold by fourteen separate, allegedly competing regional broadcasters.

Advertisers and their agencies used to obsess about each and every spot they bought, not least because many lunchtime and late night spots delivered audiences that we swoon about in peaktime nowadays. (One schedule I bought back then achieved its reach target in a single spot, a centre break of Crossroads which yielded 72 housewife TVRs, or 72% unique reach in 30 seconds albeit at only one OTS!).

This early media auditing took a while to get going, but it wasn't long before enough big advertisers were auditing to give the pools some credibility. It was boosted by the fact that (almost uniquely in the world) we have a tradition of 'publishing' broadcaster revenues into which we can divide audiences from BARB to give us average market prices. Alongside the pools these were, and are, a staple component of both media cost forecasting* and auditing.

Unsurprisingly, agencies hated auditors and often challenged them but to diminishing effect. By the mid-80s, most agencies had grudgingly accepted auditing, partly because the battle was lost and partly because there was a new front, with the new media independents leeching away our lucrative accounts for lower fee and price promises.

As auditing matured and the pools and historic databases grew, it began to offer commentary beyond pricing, evaluating schedule 'quality', cost and speed of achievement of reach and effective frequency.

By this time, media consultancy billetts – now ebiquity (lower case all round) – was a player in the space and invented the 'rack' which combined price and 'quality' measures and which still prevails today.

Later auditors sought to expand their services to offer second opinions on agencies' media plans (not too successful as I recall) and agency search and selection (a bit more successful, though also eliciting many agency allegations of improper play as they managed pitches that their own audits had sometime precipitated).

Forays into other media were not particularly auspicious. National press lent itself reasonably well to auditing even though there are more inherent variables, but magazines less so; and by the time they got to radio and posters (out-of-home to you youngsters) it was a couple of desultory slides bundled in for nothing before lunch to sweeten and maintain the auditor's client relationships. Or so I'm told.

But all the way through, auditing relied on intermediated brand advertisers – in other words those who couldn't measure the precise performance of their media from direct response data. These brands sought the surrogate comfort of knowing that they were buying 'better' than their 'peers'. (Even if sometimes everybody happened to be getting ripped off!; and by 'peers' I might mean sector competitors but more often just other advertisers of similar size and 'clout').

Sorry for the long recap, but as ever history offers some insights for today, where the three relevant defining characteristics are:

1.   Consolidation of media buying

If the assertions that there is little difference in the price at which the big agencies buy media are correct, auditing has an evolved role. It enables the advertisers, and especially the procurement people who now dominate the deals, to see how well they are performing within their agency's buying pool. Most of the smarter ones get this now.

However, a new argument has also emerged because some of the agency groups' buying pools are bigger than the auditors', so the logic goes that the buyer sometimes has bigger and better intel than the auditor.

2.   Migration away from 'interruptive' spot advertising towards 'engagement' through sponsorship, partnerships, placements, native and so on.

3.   The rise of 'digital' (sorry, that poor descriptor again)...
...neither of which lend themselves to the like-for-like comparisons which auditing offers because each instance is unique and bespoke.

Moreover, even for intermediated brands, digital channels are the ultimate performance media, throwing back huge amounts of data and partly removing the need for comparative audits. And Google and Facebook know much, much more about everybody's business and offer their own tools too – impressive if taken with an appropriate pinch of salt.

So it seems to me that auditing still has a place but is not really set for growth, at least not in the UK. Elsewhere, there is still good business to be done – in some markets, advertisers engage auditors literally to help them determine if their media plan has even been bought!

No surprise, therefore, that media consultancy is taking on a new hue. The established players are turning further towards marketing 'sciences' – return on investment, econometrics, analytics, dashboards. And latterly – and entirely logically – content verification tools which analyse delivery, viewability, safety and perhaps even financial transparency in the murky online world.

And both the established companies and some more recent entrants – some ex-auditor and some ex-agency or – client – are focusing on agency search and selection, pitch and contract advice, and best and most effective practice in the management of (probably several if not many) specialist agencies.

I should know – ISBA is also active in these spaces and we've never had so many live briefs. We're also rolling out our new model media contract, which probably won't win us any popularity contests – except amongst those we speak for.

TV commercial production consultants continue to prosper – not surprising given the costs and risk involved in many commercials and the steep rise in demand for other forms of audiovisual content. And literally as I started to write this, I learned of a new entrant in the events and out-of-home space too.

It's clear that there is a lot for advertisers to have to worry about these days, so they will seek the reassurance they need in order to have confidence in a value chain that displays some pretty 'chequered' behaviours.

Never seen that before...

Friday evening's Gogglebox was a great one with the EastEnders live murder denouement and all.

And in the first centre break, the new ad for EE's new set-top telly box, with its very competitive four-channel record and swipe functions.

It stars Kevin Bacon – and Gogglebox's own Christopher and Stephen, hairdressers of Brighton parish.

There used to be unbelievably strict rules preventing talent appearing in both ads and host programming. I once had a radio campaign shelved because my ad's voiceover was on the opposite breakfast show, for chrissakes.

Things have certainly relaxed in the 'digital' world!

*not that it helped many people in the Q1 2015!

April 2015

Wasn't Ad Week fab? (But, er, where were the clients?)

Ad Week is clearly here to stay – but it won't reach the next level unless it can attract a vital but missing constituency. So what does it need to do?

Last week's Ad Week Europe, the third such annual event, really found its stride in many ways. An incredibly busy and diverse programme over four days based around a very central venue in what many consider the greatest city in the world.

ISBA's relationship with the event started off on the wrong foot three years ago when Ad Week first descended on London at rather short notice adjacent to our Annual Conference event, compromising an important revenue source for us.

After that frosty start, bridges were rightly (re-)built and by this time round we were proud to be an 'association partner' to the event which provided:

– tickets for our members and colleagues which we duly used and peddled as widely as we could

– a speaking slot in which Gawain Owen of Nestle and I set out a new manifesto for what it means to be a premium publisher in the online age. You can see what we had to **say here**[xiv].

Speaking in the Newsroom studio, next door to but separated from the main event at BAFTA, felt a bit like we were on the fringe and not in the mainstream.

Yet despite our being opposite much bigger draws like Sir Martin Sorrell and Sir Ben Ainslie, the room was still full of some 100 delegates. And if nothing else was achieved, a job of work was done as few of them were even aware of ISBA, let alone what it does.

But in every single conversation with senior industry people, both whilst at the event and subsequently, the same question was raised: Where were the clients, the advertisers? It transpires that many commentators seem to agree on this.

I don't have the stats – organisers are incredibly jealous of their attendees and attendance stats in the online age where anything can be replicated instantaneously – so I only have my and others' impressions. And to be fair, this is an issue that dogs most industry events.

The greatest concentration was probably at the excellent lunch we co-hosted with ESI Media at Fortnum's but I know that many of them had attended a meeting at ISBA in the morning and did not linger afterwards.

Some have observed to me that a number of the event's panel sessions had suffered, with others sometimes speaking up for the clients in their absence.

Ad Week is clearly here to stay – and so it quite rightly should – but it won't reach the next level it needs to unless it can attract this vital but missing constituency. So what does it need to do?

Ever the helpful soul, I thought I'd set out my suggestions publicly so anybody can pick them up, run with them and/or work with us if they wish.

1 – Organising Committee: 48 members are listed in the conference magazine but I understand there were actually 55. Nary an advertiser nor ISBA, though, despite our recognised role as the bridge and gateway to

this sometimes reclusive constituency. Granted, competition to get senior, influential, experienced and worldly advertisers to sit on 'advisory councils' and the like is fierce – Facebook, Google, IPA to name but three – but that shouldn't and mustn't stop Ad Week.

2 – Programme: with 209 events, 113 seminars, 70 workshops over four days, it's arguably too busy, sometimes not entirely relevant and declared too late. Taking each in turn:

Five or six concurrent strands is all very well, a veritable smorgasbord offering wide choice, but...

...a number of events were admittedly interesting but not terribly relevant. For example Katie Price and Professor Brian Cox might be nice to see (and doubtless those organising wanted to meet them and they probably get good press coverage for the event) but in my conversations they didn't really ring a bell for busy clients...

...who need more notice than agency and media owner folk are perhaps used to – like a clear month.

There's clearly a need to strike a careful balance between relevance and entertainment/box office lest the event becomes pure fluff on the one hand or too dull on the other – the key here is to try and strike that balance from the client's perspective and not the industry's.

3 – Priority: This means *priority booking to all events and fast-track admission to all sessions*. "Clients aren't that special", you might say, and you'd be right, they go the bathroom just like everybody else.

But the issue here is that you want them to change their behaviour and attend the event and you need to lower any and all barriers to their consideration to achieve that.

I can tell you I wouldn't have queued all the way down BAFTA's stairs and along the street to see the Foo Fighters, let alone anyone at Ad Week.

4 – A 'safe lounge': another reason that clients are reluctant to attend is that they don't want to be mobbed or ambushed.

You might think that's the whole point of a conference, but if the paying punters aren't coming you need to think again.

The business pressures that most clients face make event attendance difficult, and their locations often exacerbate this. Most can't slip over to a nearby office between sessions or when they get called back.

So give them somewhere safe, away from random and pressured sales pitches on the fly, with a brilliant comms and meeting space so they can work and/or meet with whoever they wish to.

Two final notes. On the bright side, someone told me they'd met quite a few creatives at the event, which is good news considering current industry debate about (dis)integration and their recent reluctance towards industry fora.

But Ad Week Europe? Really? It was largely an event for and by British advertising folk with a smattering of US-based tech sales people. Though to be fair, I did meet a nice Ukrainian lady in a lift.

Outside the box

Linear TV seems to be in rude health. BARB shows healthy, if sometimes volatile, audiences and advertiser demand soared in the first quarter. Costs are on the rise, and when you talk to people you now get the sense that change may be on the way.

TV consumption is fragmenting. Is huddling round the TV to watch your family favourite show slowly sadly losing its appeal? Indicators from US colleagues suggest it might be and reports of young people watching their audiovisual content largely on handheld devices now abound.

Does the march of tech, especially domestic routers and cloud storage, suggest that we could be heading for similar change to that experienced by the music industry where content is streamed, channelled and stored on physical or virtual hubs?

Period dramas seem to be all the rage right now, prompting the thought – 'could channels further segment into specialism by programme genre?'

Would advertisers concerned with protecting their reach, frequency and costs be well-served by universal ad trading systems embracing multiple channels, platforms and devices via a single media buy? Of course, such systems would also have to guarantee brand safety from the hostile environments and fraud currently vexing online display.

With its guaranteed and certain income, the BBC is pretty well cocooned. But the imminent periodic review of its Charter and funding will see renewed and much better-founded calls for overturn of the licence fee. The tech won't be ready enough this time, but next time it will surely at last move to more equitable IP-based delivery enabling charging based on usage, not a clumsy domicile-based tax.

Me, I'm back off into the cloud myself. Until next time...

May 2015

As an adman, how should I vote?

How should the ad industry vote on May 7? Bob Wootton, director of media and advertising **at ISBA, tells** *us which box he'll be ticking.*

It's too good an opportunity to miss making a few comments around the massive decision the population is very shortly about to make.

Media comment is already frenziedly telling us that we're in uncharted political waters and that no single party will have an operating majority, so wholesale political horse-trading will follow.

And it's a very good time for some media owner revenues – notably out-of-home and the newsbrands. As Lord Tim Bell reminded us in The Telegraph recently, posters kick ass (or are at least seen to) when it comes to elections.

Marketing magazine **ran a really good piece on the parties' manifesto promises**[xv] **(I hesitate to** use the firmer word commitments, see below), so I don't need to reheat that good work here, but these are things we've highlighted as relevant to our industry from all the blurb.

Labour

...will set maximum permitted levels of sugar, salt and fat in foods marketed substantially to children.

...promise better to protect children from TV advertising of products high in sugar, fat and salt, and will ask the Committee of Advertising Practice and the Advertising Standards Authority to report on how this can be done more effectively.

...will 'crack down' on high-strength, low-cost alcohol products that 'fuel binge and underage drinking'.

The Liberal Democrats

...would also further restrict the marketing of 'junk food' to children, including restricting their advertising on TV before the 9pm watershed; maintain the effective 'Five a Day' campaign; and encourage the traffic light labelling system for food products and publication of information on calorie, fat, sugar and salt content in restaurants and takeaways.

...also propose a digital 'bill of rights' enshrining consumer privacy and support the digital single market.

...will monitor e-cigarettes carefully as a 'health' product and impose minimum pricing for alcohol.

Conservatives

...propose funding local authority public health budgets.

...would protect intellectual property by continuing to require internet service providers to block sites & proxies that carry large amounts of illegal content.

SNP

...promise minimum pricing on alcohol...and extra funding for BBC Scotland!

UKIP

...I'm told "Nothing. Absolutely nothing"!

And all parties broadly agree on:

...building out mobile coverage to ~90% of UK landmass and high-speed broadband to ~95% of UK population by 2017.

...a traffic light-based food labelling system.

...tobacco: plain packaging; kept and sold from behind counters.

...freezing the TV licence fee (aka BBC price freeze, an increased role for Ofcom and keeping Channel 4 publicly-owned.

Our political advisors suggest that, like most manifesto 'pledges' (I'm thinking tuition fees here), most of these promises could be cast aside, particularly if – as is likely – there are complex negotiations for power after the election.

It's also worth reminding ourselves that despite our undoubted and now proven contribution to the economy, employment and UK plc's leadership in e-commerce, our industry is but an eddy current in the swirl of policy promises; small change to be nickeled and dimed for greater purpose in much bigger negotiations over pensions; welfare; health, education and defence.

————————————————————

Talking of politics, the Advertising Association's recent and excellent Lead 2015 event saw calls from leading industry figures for yet greater 'responsibility', doubtless playing to Westminster sensitivities.

It also had a 'hustings' session, where Labour's Chris Bryant (fresh from a high-profile contretemps with Eton-educated singer James Blunt over privilege), Conservative Maria Miller (who resigned as Secretary of State for Culture, Media & Sport after controversial expenses) and a Liberal Democrat pitched themselves and their parties' policies.

LBC's Nick Ferrari moderated and provided the crossfire and the senior industry audience was asked to vote on who had been the most persuasive. Bryant won by a landslide – over 80% of votes – though I felt that the result was perhaps rather more an indication of the audiences' voting intentions than the merits of the arguments presented, many of which were pretty thin.

Which of course got me thinking...

One of the significant differences in the parties' pitches in this election is the so-called 'mansion tax'.

It's a Liberal Democrat conceit that has been adopted by several other parties, not least Labour, whose leader recently averred that it would be implemented 'within weeks of taking power'. Other adherents to the tax will likely jump to match his promise.

It's something you might think would be of pretty keen interest to many of our industry's leaders, many of whose success is reflected in where and what kind of home they live in. Many, many nicer houses in London and the Home Counties now tip the scales at over £2m, the widely-publicised threshold for the tax, however it might be calculated.

Then The Times tells us that people affected by the tax might also have to pay dearly themselves for 'valuation'. Pure Kafka.

Many people I know – and not only those whom it might apply – abhor the concept of and motivation behind this 'mansion tax'. People at or near the ends of successful careers or lives with diminishing incomes are amongst those likely to be affected.

They will find themselves taxed incrementally and quite arbitrarily on what could well be their only home – one for which they have worked and saved quite hard – simply because they are 'fortunate' enough to live in a goodish home in a goodish area where property prices consistently outstrip the average.

It's frankly as chilling as it is inequitable. So much for 'fairness', then.

If we are to believe what we read in the press – that the spoils are earmarked for funding things far away in a territory that is very likely vigorously to continue to seek independence from the UK in spite of its failure to vote thus when it had the opportunity recently – it just ices an already very foul-tasting cake.

So not only is this one of the most interesting and closely-fought elections of our time, but there is an issue at its core which has some parallels with the 'poll tax' of the late eighties. And we can remember what that led to.

So it will be at least as interesting to see whether people will stick to their political principles in the teeth of such a prospect.

So much for a concrete reason not to vote. Fortunately, there's a huge positive too. **The latest AA/WARC figures show that the ad economy is really bouncing back now**[xvi].

We all know – and it has now been repeatedly shown – that advertising is an effective leading indicator (or bellwether) of the economy, so the data further confirms an economic recovery that is palpable to business.

A recovery that could only have taken place through effective Government which has made hard choices in order to repair the damage left by its predecessor. Which happen to be Conservative and Labour, respectively.

You would imagine that anyone in business would subscribe to the argument – as do I – that you have to have revenue to be able to spend it; the alternative being the further borrowing which has proved so disastrous.

If you're still reading this, you're probably in little doubt as how I'll be voting on May 7. I just hope many of you will join me.

KEY

' ' – indicates a caveat and/or some cynicism

" " – indicates a quotation

June 2015

Advertising's Standing Is Being Diminished

From thoughtless and hectoring advertising on TV to the negative impact of an overly heavy ad load on the online experience, it's time the industry got its house in order, **writes ISBA's Bob** *Wootton.*

BBC radio started to report a fatal speedboat accident in Brixham harbour on May bank holiday Sunday morning, almost exactly two years after Sky executive Nick Milligan and his family were involved in a similar occurrence in Cornwall which had tragic consequences.

I have a close friend with a house and a speedboat there so I put in an urgent call and was fortunately quickly reassured. I also tried to find out more about the accident and where better than local newsbrand the Western Daily Press' website.

Information was still coming in, but the functionality of the site was not at all good. This was because the page I was looking for was stuffed full of ads, some static and clearly targeted programmatically and in real time to me, many rich media and autoplay video.

Even on my fast broadband connection these really interfered with page loading and navigation. Had I been on my mobile, it would have been quite exasperating.

It was what people call a seriously shit experience at a point when I wanted information simply and very quickly. And it really caused me to reflect on the industry we represent and how it behaves these days.

At the Advertising Association's Lead conference earlier in the year, we heard that popular favour towards advertising which had been pretty solid and static for many years is now in decline.

During the recent and long recession, I found myself noticing more and more ads resembling brochure copy, too often shouting product features with insufficient regard for viewers' interests or sentiments. I rationalised this as the consequence of an economic environment in which agencies felt forced to accede to their clients' demands for such inclusions.

We know that advertising's strongest effects can also be quite long-term and that viewers en masse are fairly inert and tolerant unless provoked, so none of this has very much effect in isolation, but when everyone's at it over sufficiently long period of time, it starts to show.

For my money, advertising's reported demise is down to two main things – too much poor, thoughtless, hectoring advertising on TV and the negative impact of an overly heavy ad load on the online experience. Especially in mobile, where usage is rising steeply.

Both have connections to a rise in supply of inventory. Granted, publishers can't get upwards of £20k for a page so easily any more – it's a couple of quid cpm instead these days. That's certainly a reason to as much of the stuff as they can, but is it a good reason?

Judging by the froth around it, everybody's obsessing with programmatic even when it's neither relevant nor applicable. But who is stepping back to really think about what they're doing, why and most importantly how it will be noticed and better-received.

Industry luminary Richard Eyre made some related observations at the same event which I bridled at in my role as one of the industry's leading advocates, but the more I reflect, the more I find myself agreeing with much of what he said.

Events haven't helped. Just recently, the mainstream press has covered:

– a major travel company's serious public relations hash of a serious compensation issue

– overly-aggressive charity marketing blamed for the demise of a civically-minded pensioner

– brand safety and ad fraud crossing into the public's awareness

– a respected US investment analyst downgrading his buy recommendations for the ad holding groups on the basis of transparency concerns

This has got to change and it's down to all of us to play our part.

Agility

I get quite a few calls from advertisers concerned about missing their TV audience targets as cost inflation returns, some of it down to declining audiences but most to resurgent advertiser demand.

It's a double-edged sword and slightly perverse – the sensitive bellwether of adspend is confirming that the economy is coming back strongly which is broadly good for business and the consumer economy, yet some people within it are missing their narrower KPIs as a result.

Meanwhile, all these calls confirm that the industry's ability to predict the market remains quite poor. A while back I raised the idea of remunerating media agencies in part on the accuracy of their forecasts and I've suggested this to a number of advertisers already.

I also commented on the annualised trading mechanism that has evolved through industry consolidation (which continues with Sky now handling

Five's airtime sales for Viacom). Perhaps it's become rather too ossified, in that it robs many budgets of their agility in the marketplace.

I'm quite surprised that no-one has weighed in yet. So come on folks, how about it?

Vlogging

I've been involved in quite a few conversations around vlogging recently.

ISBA met with Marcus Butler, the UK's #3 vlogger, recently and he impressed us – a really sorted and charming guy. We couldn't believe how much he achieves by himself – he obviously works very hard at what he loves doing.

The hot topic for vloggers and advertisers alike is how to get involved with each other. Many advertisers are dead keen to use the channel and the vloggers smell serious money. It's tough for both sides to strike what is a very delicate balance, though in my view it's even tougher for the vloggers – one step too far and they're damaged goods in the eyes of a fickle audience.

The ASA was pricked into action last year by a vlog which didn't declare Oreos' commercial interest and therefore drew some complaints. New rules were written and some guidelines issued. But now other advertisers, even those who are declaring their interest in vlogs or even launching whole branded YouTube channels, seem to be getting caught by some quite inconsistent interpretation by the ASA Council.

It's not the first time advertisers have been caught by the industry's self-regulator learning to cope with new environments on the job, and the ASA isn't in a popularity contest, but its credibility will be challenged if it doesn't get its story straight.

Corruption

The dawn raids on senior FIFA personnel represent a new and graver chapter of a saga that has been rumbling with increasing vigour for some time.

Readers and friends (you know who you are, let's meet in the phone box on the corner of Trafalgar Square later) will know that I have a near-total sport bypass so I hesitate to weigh in. But the relevance, adjacency to our industry and number of players common to both require that I do.

The major global brand sponsors are absolutely right to resurface and escalate the concerns they have been expressing for some time. Even if they stop short of pulling out for now and settle for words like reassess, review, reconsider and perhaps even suspend, protraction can't be good for them and their brands' reputations.

Withdrawal would be a very public way of (re)asserting their own probity.

The sponsors... and their position

Top-tier

ADIDAS
"Monitoring the situation"

COCA-COLA
"Monitoring the situation"

HYUNDAI
"Concerned with the situation"

GAZPROM
"No comment"

VISA
"We expect Fifa to take swift and immediate steps to address these issues within its organisation"

Total amount top-tier partners paid Fifa in 2014
$177m

Figures not available for value of individual sponsorship deals but top-tier Fifa partners pay between $24m and $44m a year

Second-tier

MCDONALD'S
"Taking the situation very seriously"

BUDWEISER
"Monitoring the situation"

Total amount second-tier sponsors paid in 2014
$131m

National supporters
Consists of a maximum of 20 sponsors, 4 in each region who back their domestic competitions

$46m in 2014

Source: Fifa

Fifa revenue 2011-14
$5.7bn

- TV rights **$2.48bn**
- Marketing rights (including sponsors) **$1.63bn**
- Other **$1.61bn**

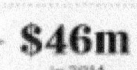

Courtesy The Times, 29-5-15

Broadcasters will be even more torn over potentially severing links with the ultimate prime content asset.

But am I alone in seeing parallels we would be wise to pay some attention to? I've written before and will doubtless do so again on advertiser concerns around transparency. Like the FIFA issue, there's blanket denial from the perpetrators and tracing transgressions is fraught.

Any conversation on said topic usually quickly moves to how lucky we are that our game is so clean in this market. We often flatter ourselves, though there's little doubt that it's far worse in many other markets and the US are now finally cottoning on to just how flawed their market is too.

But many of the issues – undisclosed rebates and kickbacks, beautiful Kentish kitchens etc – are similar. Just saying.

July 2015

Making sense of the global pitch frenzy

From Coca-Cola to Sony, more global media business is up for grabs than at any previous time. What does this mean, and how should we interpret it?

So our summer's finally arrived with some really hot weather, and everybody's attention rightly turns to grabbing a couple of weeks of well-earned rest, probably with their loved ones and perhaps somewhere far away from the daily routine.

Just as naturally, agency managers' attention turns to making sure their forts are sufficiently-well manned over the holidays so that they can run what is often a very day-to-day business.

Clients, whose rhythms tend to be more regular, often like to put key projects out before they break and then review them on their return. Key projects like their media accounts, for example.

This summer is seeing the mother of all pitch frenzies. You surely can't have missed the news reports which cumulatively show that more global media business is up for grabs than at any previous time. MAD – Mediapost Agency Daily – calls it a tsunami of pitches.

P&G, Coca-Cola, VW group, Unilever, Sony, Coty, L'Oreal and 21st Century Fox are all reported to be reviewing. These are all big accounts, operating in dozens, if not hundreds, of markets. The review processes will be as Byzantine, widespread and probably protracted as their marketing activities necessarily are.

So – opportunity, or headache? Well both, of course, but I'd argue mainly the latter. But first, why all these reviews now?

Some – but not all – are statutory. Maybe not in Greece, but in many markets the money is coming back so companies are once again moving out of retrenched, defensive positions into innovation and attack mode.

Markets and consumers are changing, demanding different things. Usually more quickly and cheaply. Internet connectedness is now ubiquitous, particularity in developed markets. It's no longer "are you connected?" but "how do you connect?" and the answer is increasingly "on the go".

Yet brands, the lifeblood of ad revenues, are still incredibly important, whether trusted household staples or – just look to the Far East – premium brands and labels.

The routes advertisers take to market are changing too. TV has held up amazingly well as the channel of choice for major, category-leading brands, but the tech-based routes are now the biggest global plays by far and they are looking a little bit less shiny than hitherto.

Serious concerns over viewability, brand safety, anti-fraud, transparency of the complex value chain and now ad blocking are all taking their toll.

Fresh from this year's Cannes shindig, a leading industry commentator's view was that it has now been ruined by the combination of clients and tech companies seeking the most global and direct relations they can get with the former.

I find it hard to tell whether this view is just la recherche du temps perdu or something we should be concerned about. But I will offer once again in my po-faced style that some of our industry leaders' endless selfies of jollies do not befit 'business leaders'.

Advertisers' relationships with those who help them craft their communications are also shifting. This is partly because the new always-on crowdsourceable world has disintermediated the value chain. And partly because, just when advertisers need reliable, honest, capable partners to help them navigate an increasingly complicated world, instead they're coming not to trust them so much.

This is not to say that they don't trust the teams who create and place advertising day-to-day. In my experience they do, and I'll venture my personal opinion here – they should.

No, it's month to month and year to year we should be worrying about and that's in the hands of the business managers – and increasingly those who trade the big bulk media deals.

The US advertiser organisation, the ANA (Association of National Advertisers) holds a very well-attended Commercial Issues Conference event for its members (a who's who in corporate America where most marketing decision originates) each spring.

Last year saw the US client world experience a sort of slow-motion damascene conversion as they realised that all was not well in their own backyard. (They'd suspected everything was a bit fishy everywhere else for some time, of course). This year's built on that, with transparency taking such a prominent stance that a joint client-agency task force was set up to try and get to the bottom of things.

Ambitious as it might sound, we should watch how that goes with the keenest interest. There have already been a few murmured calls for a similar initiative in the UK.

And no surprise, business issues from online accountability and transparency to payment terms (yes, those again) are central to these global reviews. There are simply so many local variables on global business that it makes sense to sort out the big issues common to many, if not all, markets.

So these are the underlying reasons. The big question posed earlier in this piece is whether the agencies can actually respond effectively. One major global pitch is a serious undertaking – and cost – for an agency or holding group. Several at once, well...

There are only a small number of networks really capable of handling such accounts and there are only so many top teams within each, almost certainly fewer than the accounts up for grabs. So for the first time in my long recollection, this means that we're going to see tier-two teams pitching for tier-one global business.

Each pitch will be looking for improved value too, begging a really big question: how do agencies that have made an art form of playing value off between their clients extract yet more value above that which they already claim – without going yet further underground?

The sharp-eyed amongst you might spot that I've managed to get this far without referring to the natural tensions between marketing and procurement disciplines. Vigorous, sometimes rather blinkered but undoubtedly focused procurement has a heavy hand in the situation all advertisers and their partners find themselves in today. It won't get them out of it.

The advertisers will need all the help they can get, but from whom? The only answer lies in the small band of professional advisors who sit in the leading national and international advertiser trade associations – yes, like

ISBA – and an even smaller band of specialist consultants, many of them also based in London.

So it looks like it could be a busy summer for us too. Cancel all leave? Steady on.

August 2015

The contradictions within the programmatic claim

We should be more mindful of the language we use when talking about programmatic ad trading.

In my admittedly rather overlong experience of the ad industry, I've learned that it loves nothing more than to seize upon the new and jump aboard bandwagons and their attendant jargon. It's often been said that for an industry which claims innovation as its lifeblood, it's terribly conservative.

The bandwagon it's on right now is both one of the most pervading and the most runaway I can recall (since 'media-neutral planning' – RIP – or 'bought, owned, earned', that is). And the jargon out there is in a league of its own, believe me!

I come from a time when Prog meant embarrassingly long, complex and often incomprehensible pieces of music delivered with virtuosity, show and pomp to a mainly stoned audience.

To the current generation of marketers and media folk out there it means something entirely different.

Programmatic – Prog to its friends – promises to deliver the Holy Grail of the right message in front of the right person in the right place at the right time. Even the right mood. In doing so, it also promises to clarify, simplify and make transparent.

Sound too good to be true? Yup.

Instead, we have a fog of evangelists, technologists, more conferences than you can shake a fistful of sticks at and yet still a whole lot of confusion.

I had a moment of clarity at a private event ISBA held for its members recently, where TubeMogul and Adjust Your Set delivered two really excellent presentations on different facets of the convergent space between TV and online.

The flash of clarity was that too many people are enthusing (good news) but not using sufficiently accurate language and thereby confusing, bemusing and even misleading (bad news).

A number of the leading advertisers then started hitting me with a riff that's been going round in my head for some time. It comes from a question – how can a billboard or a primetime TV spot be 'programmatic'.

Programmatic has been sold with some gusto as the marketer's equivalent of a very sharp needle whose tip can be placed (increasingly in real time) on a very specific target consumer. (Pace privacy hounds – not a named individual but a very accurately described type of person).

Granularity is the watchword, and very sexy it is too. Yet Prog is now claiming to be the saviour of media which are intrinsically massive too. That is, they reach many people at once, and/or quite indiscriminately.

Indeed, the common frame of reference, aka 'the watercooler moment', is their charm and their lure. Think of ITV's and latterly Thinkbox's work on the value of fame, widely subscribed to by many big advertisers serving large and mass markets.

These media are inherently not granular, rather their appeal is in the aggregate. So how can they practically be traded programmatically in any useful sense?

This is where we get into trouble with loose language. What I think the perps mean is not programmatic but automated.

(Businesspeople once swapped long division for log tables and slide rules; then calculators for slide rules; and then began to adopt computers in the 70s. Each reduced the amount of time spent on iterative processes. The promise was that the time thus released could be re-purposed for higher things, though that's not quite how things turned out but that's for another day/another column).

Full automation of trading promises this in spades, and it's happening all over the place.

But it's not Prog. Granted, Prog requires an automated environment in which to work, but is itself a specific subset of automation.

I completely get how mass media can be traded and refined automatically, but nobody has yet managed to explain to me how they can realistically be traded to the point that Prog proselytises. I've asked and will continue to, but so far all I get is people running for cover, not answers.

More recent Prog pitches, particularly from independent specialist players which claim no media ownership or brokerage layer, argue that Prog will hound out the multiple layers that have grown up in the online media value chain, each of which takes its dip into the money as it passes through, reportedly leaving less than half of it for the working media the advertiser thinks they're buying.

This argument plays extremely well to advertisers, be they those obsessed with their targeting or those concerned by the many well-documented issues emerging in the online space, not least transparency.

So my conclusion is that we should all use language more carefully in this area. The current obsession with Prog does not tell the whole story.

Automation is good too, and a much more relevant descriptor of a lot of what is going on, so let's use each where it applies and not try and attach Prog to everything from your morning espresso to a truly granular media buy.

None of this is to say, of course, that the general direction of travel isn't towards the more granular and targetable. Media buyers can leverage 4OD's 12 million signed up users' data and target them more accurately than ever before. But wherever it's going, 4OD still contributes but a small fraction of Channel 4's revenues.

Similarly, Sky's AdSmart can now put targeted messages into 500,000 of its 12 million subscriber homes. So far, it's got down to postcode district and will be even more remarkable when it goes deeper, first to postcode sector. But folks – it still won't be Prog. My and many postcodes embrace multiple buildings comprising more dwellings and yet more diverse individuals.

Bus shelters with recognition software or nascent interactive features support some basic elements of Prog, but roadside or precinct panels? Too many people pass them – which is a good thing!

Why is this of any consequence? Well, simply because every time you lob Prog into your presentation where it doesn't fit in the mind of the listener, you lose your prospect's comprehension and attention. Which is not good for business.

September 2015

BBC woes, pushbacks on programmatic and mobile ad-blocking

ISBA's director of media & advertising, Bob Wootton, gives his views on the top priorities for media and advertising.

BBC Charter – Adios BBC Trust?

A lot of press right now around the BBC's future in the light of the imminent review of the 10-year Government Charter which defines its purpose, scope, and activities.

There's a strong focus on the effectiveness and future of the BBC Trust, which has not distinguished itself as successor to the discredited BBC Governors that went before it. No wonder other solutions are being considered.

Indeed, the Trust appears to be seriously sidelined already, as Chancellor Osborne and Culture Secretary Whittingdale negotiate directly with BBC DG Lord Hall, for example on sacrificing services to fund free licences for the over 75s.

Hopefully this Charter Review will be more cognizant of the rate and scale of change in the media and will act accordingly.

Pushbacks on programmatic 1 – Tech runs for the bushes

I'm pleased to report that my previous outpourings on programmatic excited some lively comment.

Apparently programmatic is the only future, the pinpoint targeting it provides eclipsing all other media channel pretenders. But if that's the case, why does everybody I know (at least, the small subset that even notices online ads) complain about being stalked for weeks by advertisers of things they've just bought?

Yes, they already bought the computer/blender/razor/whatever but surely the omnipotent internet can offer them other products.

I'm also less pleased to report that most respondents make all too quickly for the bushes of tech detail. It's getting hard to find people to engage with on the overarching drivers of the issues that our industry faces.

Pushbacks on programmatic 2 – So what's really in it for who?

When I've interrogated some of the pushback I've had about my comments on prog, or more precisely automation, two things surface.
Media owners are embracing it partly because everybody else is, and partly because it promises to enable them to sell their long tail of inventory. What we used to call the 'crap' back in the day.

Agencies likewise, but with the motivation that it already delivers massive margin hikes and will bring further efficiency and enable costly headcount reduction. Fascinatingly, neither of these are in any way connected to what their advertiser customers say they want.

P.s. Talking of prog, I went to see the latest incarnation of old prog faves King Crimson at the Hackney Empire recently. Outstanding.

Ad blocking...

...has emerged as a clear and present danger and a major talking point. A well-attended event organised by ATS at the Queen Elizabeth Hall served to remind us of the clear fissures between industry, especially publishers, ad blockers (e.g. AdBlock Plus, Shine etc.) and adblocker blockers (e.g. SourcePoint).

The 'old compact' between advertiser and consumer revolved around the moot/implicit understanding that most of the media and content wouldn't exist without the subsidy from the ads, so they were – as Jeremy Bullmore wisely offers – uninvited but fortunately relatively benign guests, and therefore tolerated.

This is being stretched online as the media owners, faced with getting pennies from digital whereas they used to see pounds from, say, paper, are trying to sustain their revenues by stuffing their pages with lots of holes for ads.

Meanwhile, the advertisers entirely understandably wish for their ads to be noticed and engaged with and therefore prefer richer media executions over dumb and easily ignored banners.

These richer media ads consume more bandwidth, especially in quantity, so they are slowing the viewing experience, especially when readers do not have a fast connection. Frustration with these slowed page loading speeds and not a general hatred of ads is surely the main driver of the now worryingly widespread adoption of adblocking softwares.

These have themselves also evolved into very user-friendly apps which only take a couple of clicks to install.

Once again, the internet has brought disintermediation and empowerment to consumers. However, amidst all this, the basic 'compact' still just about holds.

Where it gets really troubling in my view is mobile. Not only are screens necessarily too small to be hospitable to ad interventions, but the downloading of uninvited ads consumes bandwidth, depleting whatever monthly data allowance users have opted for, in turn sometimes preventing them from further accessing the content they seek unless they pay to top up their data allowance.

In other words, they are now de facto having to pay to receive uninvited guests, breaking the established 'compact'.

With the launch of a new Apple operating system with integrated adblocking, we would do well to pay this some attention now, lest the meaning of that much vaunted 'year of mobile' phrase turns from 'when will it actually lift off?' to 'well, it lasted about a year and then tanked'.

Media 2020

ISBA held a joint event with MediaSense last week at which the results of research amongst leading advertisers on their attitudes towards the media future were unveiled. Several interesting themes emerged, but two stood out.

Advertisers are now actively exploring in-boarding services they have previously outsourced, especially those closest to the customer interface like social and Customer Relationship Management.

They also continue to rate creative agencies' contribution to/of big ideas, but are now widely questioning their role beyond that. Media agencies' role in implementing legacy media remains unquestioned, but their role beyond that is in serious question and subject to frequent challenge.

Core to this is resolving being a 'trusted advisor' against the palpable tendency from agent towards vendor. And as long as agencies' declared profits bear decreasing resemblance to their known margins, advertisers will be ever more skeptical. Agencies face an uncertain future.

At last – a BBH ad that isn't dressed for dinner

You might like or leave some individual ad executions, but BBH has always been rightly famous not only for the strategy underpinning but also the finish of its ads.

So imagine my surprise to open my paper copy of the Sunday Times magazine and see the front page spread for Audi's Q7 tub. The ad itself wouldn't trouble my own hall of fame, but it was something else that struck me.

The cover of the magazine is a different weight and finish of paper to the body. As the first spread, this ads straddles both substrates, so the left hand page's background is palpably whiter and the right hand yellower. (OK, so the scan above doesn't really show this to best advantage but I couldn't miss under domestic tungsten lighting).

Perhaps this reflects the modern fashion to decouple the production chain, but it would surely never have been allowed out like this in Big Hegsy's day?

Tweeting, part 99

People's Twitter feeds remain as bemusing as ever, especially when they're projected at events. The same ATS event saw a fair amount of flaming, an attempted feminist takeover quelled, but the cake was taken by speaker tweets telling us they were on their way to address us. That's all right then.

October 2015

The five horsemen of the digital apocalypse

Unsafe, unviewable, fraudulent, blocked and badly targeted... How can advertisers overcome an increasingly challenging digital landscape?

The shiny promises of extreme targeting, high relevance and zero wastage seem to be wearing through to reveal a far less savoury reality in online media. Not a day passes for me without a conversation with a major advertiser about at least one, if not more, of these concerns.

On viewability, I've been accused of not being clear enough or leading the charge as I should, so let me set that straight.

I don't see why any advertiser in their right mind should target anything less than the 100% viewability that all other media offer. (Remember, this is viewability, not viewing. As long as a TV commercial is broadcast, a press ad published or a billboard posted, they are viewable).

To be quite fair to publishers, they do a lot to prevent unsafe ad placements, but the job is never-ending. In an online world where there is plenty of media choice everyone should consider themselves as good only as their last action. Serve an ad in an unsafe place and you should lose the business. Yes, even Facebook. Simples.

Similarly, any publisher or network with any self-respect and calling itself 'premium' should undertake unconditionally to repel any fraudulent connection whatsoever (and to cycle any windfall receipts perversely arising straight back into mechanisms to detect and eradicate further fraud).

I've written before on the apparent paradoxes within online. The tensions between rampant claims of pinpoint targeting and relevance jar with the emerging realities of un- or poorly-targeted advertising. Reports of very disappointing targeting, even through some of the companies claiming to lead the field, are now reaching me. I'll be exploring this further with some vigour anon.

Likewise, the nonsense of retargeted ads stalking people who have already bought stuff. It's an affront to good advertising practice, old world or new, and tarnishes what's left of industry's reputation. It stinks and should stop henceforth. If only.

For several years now, advertisers concerned with these various shortcomings have had to engage and pay themselves for the content verification solutions which surface them.

In the early days, I argued that advertisers should be prepared to fund the exploratory stage and prime the pump for the day when their partners would need to move beyond reassurance and provide proof of viewability, safety, authenticity of inventory, and effective targeting.

I had expected that day to be with us by now, but it isn't.

So a call out as it's overdue – I humbly suggest that any media owner looking to enjoy an advertiser's patronage should now underpin their pitch with the reassurance of mutually-agreed content verification from JICWEBS' accredited list of providers.

All this said, advertisers have an important part to play too. They will have to be tougher and more resolute to drive these necessary changes through. If not, those further along the value chain will continue to make hay. And who can blame them? In these days of 'minimum viable product' (really hate that notion), business is business after all.

But lest I appear unreasonable, let me turn to the serious challenges of fraud and ad blocking, much tougher nuts to crack.

I can't get my head round how fraudulent impressions generated by bots unwittingly installed on millions of users' devices and which learn and imitate users' behaviour can be convincingly detected, isolated and removed. So I'm very glad there are many far smarter people than me applying themselves to the challenge and I really hope they get somewhere soon.

And as for ad blocking, we as an industry claim to obsess with 'listening to the consumer'. But we aren't. What I'm observing is those same consumers, who do not get up in the morning thinking that they must install an ad blocker, being driven to do so in their millions by our behaviours.

Too many ads, not relevant enough, poorly targeted, using bandwidth-hungry rich media, autoloads and so on are interfering with and slowing the online user experience.

And to borrow from my fellow Mediatel columnist Dominic **Mills' recent piece**[xvii], "if advertisers are pumping out, let's put it this way, bottom-of-the-funnel shit into dirt-cheap media on an industrial scale, then they're not going to either afford or bother with better creative".

No wonder users are installing ad blocker apps which take but two clicks to get up and running. Even worse in mobile, where these ads take over precious screen space and squander people's data allowances and their battery life – the three biggest issues for them.

Ad blocking is here to stay – indeed, a tech arms race where blockers are blocked by blocker blockers, blocker blockers by blocker blocker blockers, and so on, seems to be in prospect.

I see solutions in two areas:

1. Moderation of the current frenzy to stuff everything full of (sometimes poor) ads, and;

2. Re-establishing an understanding with consumers that their tolerating and sometimes viewing and even acting on the ads funds the content they value and seek.

Hence my rooting for ITV, Channel 4, The Washington Post and any other publisher that declines to serve content to people running ad blockers.

I do, however, think that the right form of words has yet to be found – hopefully one that gets into the public's consciousness just like "other magazines are available" did when the BBC was required to qualify the promotion of its own titles on its TV channels. Try this...

"We're sorry that we can't serve you what you've asked for. The content on this site relies on advertising for its funding, but we've detected that you might be using some kind of ad blocking software.

We'd much rather deliver your request, so kindly go into your ad blocker's settings and either disable it or add us to your 'whitelist'.

Thanks.

It might just be me...

I get invited to a fair number of evening events, many hosted by or for companies that seek a higher profile amongst clients and agencies. Yes, they eat into precious personal time, but they're usually pretty smart affairs at nice venues with good food and drink, often moderated by a well-qualified table host, where I might get to learn something.

In truth, like all events, some are better than others, the better ones usually reflecting greater attention to detail in their organisation. Things like ambient noise (which hampers effective conversation), number of courses served (the arrival and inevitable ceremonious introduction of each of which interrupts flow).

But what's really striking me lately is the level of conversation. Dinner used to be a time for some pretty wide-ranging and high-level discussion but these days everybody runs straight for the cover of detail. In my experience, people involved in data are the worst, apparently unable to see the wood for the trees at all and frankly pretty stultifying company.

If they're the future, it's going to be a dull one. I thought it might just be me getting long in the tooth, but the more people I talk to about it, the more I realise that (many) others hold the same view.

On the bright side, knowing this at least I'll get some of my evenings back and maybe even lose a few pounds too.

November 2015

Bring In The Spooks

The US investigation into media rebates could now impact the UK – and precipitate a wholesale recalibration of remuneration and what is considered legitimate practice, writes ISBA's Bob Wootton.

A couple of weeks ago, ISBA's US counterpart (the ANA, or Association of National Advertisers) announced that it had appointed two firms to investigate media rebates and transparency issues, such were the concerns of its advertiser members.

As the next-largest and most influential advertiser body in the world, a lot of eyes swiftly turned to what we at ISBA might be doing in the UK so I thought it might be useful to set out some background before looking at implications and consequences.

- - -

Transparency and rebates, visible or hidden, have been a familiar part of many countries' media trading conversations for over 20 years, but it seems that they were less well-recognised in the US.

That all changed abruptly at the ANA's May 2014 Advertising Financial Management conference in Naples, Florida, attended by some 700 advertiser delegates, where one Jon Mandel, previously CEO of MediaCom US, **spilt the beans**[xviii]. ANA had also conducted some research amongst advertisers.

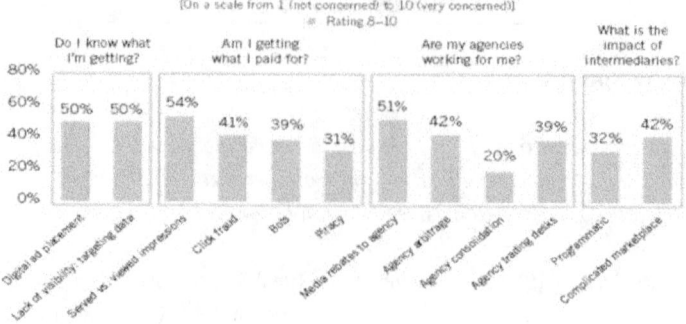

Source: March 2014, "ANA/Forrester Research Evolution of the Media Buying Industry" survey

My ISBA colleague Debbie Morrison was speaking and avers that the atmosphere was pretty electric for such an event. In a single day, denial gave way to discovery, concern, even anger.

Fast forward to this year's event, again in May but this time in Phoenix Arizona (they do hold these events in rather nice places) which naturally revisited the subject.

Rightly anticipating keen delegate interest, ANA had worked behind the scenes to establish a joint task force with the American Association of Advertising Agencies (usually known as the 4A's), which was announced at the event.

Delegates seemed satisfied that something was indeed happening. Invitations to tender and a request for proposals from relevant 'research partners' were issued, almost two dozen responses were received and meetings were held with about a dozen of the more promising ones.

(WPP trading arm Group M's global CEO Irwin Gottlieb also spoke, albeit in very measured tones by all accounts – Tom Denford of IDComms was there and **reported on the event**[xix]).

Somewhere along the line ANA moved forward alone, then, in October, announced that it had **appointed ebiquity and K2**[xx].

We all know ebiquity and its compliance subsidiary, Firm Decisions, but what about K2? It turns out that it is the second business to be set up by one Jules A Kroll.

His first, **Kroll Inc.**[xxi], established in 1972, is the world's largest corporate investigations and risk consulting firm. **K2 Intelligence**[xxii], launched in 2009, is his new(er) challenger brand in the same space and styles itself as "an investigative and integrity consulting firm".

These are very serious companies indeed. They advise their mainly corporate, multinational clients on all matters of security, from setting up facilities and making their employees safe in new and sometimes hostile territories, to cyber security.

They recruit from the police, armed forces and intelligence services as often as the accounting, legal and consulting professions. Their services also don't come at all cheap.

Press coverage suggests that the investigation may not be confined to the US alone.

− − −

I've spent quite a bit of time this year thinking how we might best pursue a similar agenda for our members. With my knowledge of just how deep media and compliance auditing firms can currently reach, I started from a rather skeptical place.

My lightbulb moment came when I was chatting to an old bandmate who now heads up a big region for Kroll Inc. and almost accidentally started asking him 'whether his firm did this kind of thing'. At last I had found the combination of tools I might need. Great minds must think alike, because it transpires that, quite independently, the ANA had reached the same conclusion.

Every agency I know claims it doesn't sell itself down the river, simultaneously bemoaning its competitors' suicidally-predatory pricing."

The question which drives all this is a really simple one. "How can our agency 'partners' be posting margins which are not only rather greater than ours, (far from a sin, much more a reflection of a well-run business) but many times greater than what we know we and most others are paying them (Ouch)?"

_ _ _

So what are the implications of all this? Well, the 4A's withdrawal indicates that ANA is unlikely to get any agency help in its quest. Sir Martin Sorrell, chief executive of the world's biggest agency holding group, WPP, has already **implied otherwise**[xxiii], but I'd still expect agencies to play hardball.

Even with a K2 on board, things will surely pivot on the contracts which the advertisers have in place. That could be tricky.

From our own extensive work in the space, we know that despite our persistent encouragement, too few clients have really comprehensive and up-to-date contracts in place and fewer still have the crucial reach to probe the agency holding groups where many deals are done. Our understanding is that it's no better and perhaps rather worse in the US.

Many advertisers report to us that they find the extremely protracted negotiations with their agencies too painful and distracting to pursue indefinitely. But whether a suitable contract is or is not in place, agency refusal to answer admittedly probing questions will signal confirmation to their clients that they do indeed have something (maybe plenty) to hide.

This will do nothing to rekindle the 'trusted partner' status agencies claim to crave, but which many have in truth already largely foregone by taking rebates and by becoming media vendors in their own rights.

No, agencies will surely resist this investigation vigorously because their very income is at stake. They certainly can't make nearly enough to meet their owners' demands for volume and margin growth from what their clients actually pay them, even though they themselves have been instrumental in driving those very incomes through the floor.

Jenny Biggam of The Seven Stars offered a valuable contribution to this debate just this week with a letter to *Campaign* in which she said agencies should not blame clients for their own transgressions.

Every agency I know claims it doesn't sell itself down the river, simultaneously bemoaning its competitors' suicidally-predatory pricing, but my conversations with advertisers suggest that pretty much everybody's at it. (Sir Martin also joined this conversation **this week**[xxiv]. 'Insane' would surely have more pertinent meaning than 'inane', but perhaps that would have opened him up to litigation.)

As for the media owners, it's an open secret that many, even amongst the biggest, are deeply concerned about the concentration of power that now lies with media agencies, so they could be quietly rooting for the lid to be lifted off things.

We continue to keep very close to our US colleagues so that we can keep our advertiser members informed and they can decide what action they might want us to take.

Just as ad-blocking is perhaps the 'extinction event' that could finally cause the industry to refrain from its excesses online, so this investigation could perhaps precipitate a wholesale recalibration of remuneration and what is considered legitimate practice.

Or, as my fellow columnist **Dominic Mills has already suggested**[xxv], it could simply end up being buried in a massive round of face-saving.

Watch this space...

I don't often deal in certainties, but here's one.

We so haven't heard the last of ad-blocking. **This**[xxvi] just in courtesy of Paul Wright at Apple takes the biscuit. Is anyone out there still in denial about the harm we are wreaking in consumers' eyes?

Update from the editor:

This article was updated on Thursday 19 November at 9am. The original said the 4A's had withdrew from the task force, leaving the ANA to 'paddle its own canoe'. The 4A's maintain they had offered to participate in the selection of the agency.

"While the 4A's favored the continuity and effectiveness of our joint efforts, the ANA has decided to move forward with its solo sponsorship of a fact-finding initiative into agency media practices," a 4A's statement said. "The 4A's will continue to collaborate with ANA on media transparency to the fullest extent feasible."

December 2015

A rather serious thought at a rather frivolous time of year

It has been an eventful year in advertising – so here ISBA's Bob Wootton joins up the dots and leaves us with his closing remarks.

During the aftermath of the recent Paris atrocities, we saw the Belgian law enforcement agencies successfully asking citizens and the media alike to delay their social media posts so as not to alert the terrorist perpetrators to their actions in real time.

It worked, with many people looking to 'break' Twitter by posting pictures of cats in support instead. Afterwards, the police followed up by expressing their thanks with a picture of a bowl of cat food. Modern and brilliant.

This story further emphasises how important social media, especially Twitter, have become to news gathering and dissemination. And a reminder of just how essential they have become to terrorists and others who do not wish their fellow humans well.

Public debate rages across the world as to whether law enforcement agencies should have greater powers to 'listen' to social media channels.

Governments tend to argue that they must, while the channels themselves supported by civil liberties lawyers and other members of the liberal intelligentsia tend to argue otherwise.

Google, Facebook, Twitter et al are commercial companies whose stocks are publicly traded. Their valuations are geared closely to their subscriber numbers and their attendant ad revenues.

Advertisers continue to spend very serious amounts of money in these channels despite the emergence of the shortcomings in the digital media space which have now been well documented.

What would happen if there was a movement, perhaps initiated by right-leaning newspapers, encouraging social media users to unsubscribe from social channels that did not allow authorities better access for preventing heinous crimes?

All have significant numbers of dormant and very infrequent users to whom this would mean little inconvenience, let alone hardship.

And what if individual advertisers who have a deep vested interest in democratic civil society and protecting its values also chose to exercise their choice in a competitive market?

Call this an extension of the Corporate Social Responsibility so many wear on their sleeves. Perhaps even give it a snappy new name – Corporate *Societal* Responsibility.

Just a thought.

Schmercentages

The latest bliptrend seems to be to tell everyone what percentage is the optimum to spend here, there and everywhere.

At Google/YouTube's spectacular, well-attended and doubtless expensive Brandcast event in October, we had statuesque UK MD Eileen Naughton telling us that 24% of all TV budgets should now be going on YouTube.

Nice try, but of course that will elicit plenty of legitimate challenge from the likes of our excellent and always excitable Thinkbox and its broadcaster members.

A fair list of other media owners is joining in too – not surprising as they all resent Google for stealing so much of their lunch through its almost complete domination of the supply of the marketers' crack cocaine, Search. Competition and Markets Authority, anybody?

And more recently, we heard that we should be spending 45% of out-of-home budgets on digital displays. Yes, the media owners are understandably seeking to recoup their significant investment in these much more impressive but also more expensive displays, which they have obviously located at all their most prime locations.

And from what I can gather, they do really pull in the revenue.

But this is not rigorous media planning. Before we know it, we'll all be spending several hundred per cent of our budgets to these entirely spurious 'norms'.

In a sense, this is a direct descendent of the way much media is traded on volume and share commitments instead of merit.

The media industry has been leeching some of its most talented planners as they realise that their carefully-crafted comms plans are hardly worth the paper they're printed on as they get bent far out of shape once they're fed into holding groups' trading systems.

Another unintended consequence is that advertisers seek – and media owners can increasingly provide – agile solutions. Yet annual group deals hamper such agility, especially towards year-end.

Meanwhile, auditors tell me that they still regularly see 'media plans' with a line and a (usually hefty) budget for 'programmatic'. And digital agency folk counter with some stinging criticism of auditors' digital offerings.

Reminder: 'programmatic' is a way of trading, not a channel. Doubtless we'll continue to see too much emphasis on self-interested iteration and not enough on going back to first principles and considering what it is we're trying to do by advertising in the first place.

Hell's teeth, we could even take a leaf out of Apple's book – the largest company in the world spends nearly all its ad budgets in 'old-school' media.

Ironic?

A recent **online newspaper article**[xxvii] about the hacking of billboard sites during the recent Paris Climate Summit is a prime example of the problem with current online advertising – too many highly-invasive ads all over the place, greatly hampering reading and navigation.

The page reads great with an adblocker. No wonder adblocking is gaining ground – there simply has to be a better way than this and the sooner the whole ad industry engages on it substantively and constructively the better.

Then over the weekend I was trying to find a recent but unsatisfactory purchase which I'm challenging on my eBay, only for the thing I was looking for to be obscured by a persistent skyscraper overlay from a very well-known high-street bank.

Grr. It's my job to defend advertising but I honestly find these hard to defend and am genuinely surprised at reputable companies presenting stuff like this.

Acknowledgements

It's customary to thank those without whom etc.

So thanks to my long-suffering wife and celebrity florist Liz Inigo Jones and my son Cal who's about to embark on his own career in the UK's world-leading creative industries.

Also to my colleagues at ISBA, especially proofreaders Mario Yiannacou and Hicham Felter, and the guys at MediaTel – Managing Director Derek Jones and Newsline Editor David Pidgeon – for publishing me in the first place.

Bob Wootton
London, January 2016

References

[i] http://mediatel.co.uk/newsline/2013/12/04/am-i-allowed-to-rant-trading-desks-debate-transparency/

[ii] http://mediatel.co.uk/newsline/2013/10/28/ipa-fifth-of-agencies-experience-negative-pitch-process/

[iii] http://www.pinkbike.com/news/video-cal-wootton-2013-Showreel.html

[iv] http://www.mediaweek.co.uk/article/1292758/trading-desks-independents-answer-client-concerns

[v] http://mediatel.co.uk/newsline/1996/06/03/conference-report-admaps-bonfire-of-the-jics/

[vi] http://thinkboxblog.brandrepublic.com/2014/07/18/advertisings-dirty-laundry/

[vii] http://mediatel.co.uk/newsline/2014/07/21/toxic-cesspit-of-online-fraud-and-mec-top-of-the-class/

[viii] http://www.ft.com/cms/s/0/788d6d42-da6c-11e3-8273-00144feabdc0.html?siteedition=uk#axzz37vWSMewz

[ix] http://adcontrarian.blogspot.co.uk/2014/07/the-dumbest-people-on-earth.html

[x] http://decipherconsultancy.wordpress.com/2014/09/08/the-implications-of-scottish-independence-on-the-uk-tv-industry/

[xi] http://www.mirror.co.uk/news/uk-news/big-six-hold-times-energy-3168050

[xii] http://mediatel.co.uk/newsline/2014/10/06/ad-fraud-driven-by-poor-procurement-culture-says-vivaki-boss/

[xiii] http://badassadvertisingjobtitles.com/

[xiv] http://advertisingweek.eu/replay/#date=2015-03-24~video-id=292~venue=10%20

[xv] http://www.marketingmagazine.co.uk/article/1343033/manifestos-marketers-tory-labour-lib-dem-green-ukip-promises-brands

[xvi] http://mediatel.co.uk/newsline/2015/04/21/aawarc-digital-sends-uk-advertising-to-its-highest-growth-in-four-years/

[xvii] http://mediatel.co.uk/newsline/2015/10/12/i-used-to-sneer-at-creative-programmatic-but-now/

[xviii] http://adage.com/article/agency-news/mediacom-ceo-mandel-skewers-agencies-incentives/297470/

[xix] http://idcomms.com/2015-ana-advertising-financial-management-conference-a-consultants-view/

[xx] http://uk.businessinsider.com/ana-hires-k2-intelligence-and-ebiquity-to-conduct-media-transparency-and-rebates-study-2015-10?pundits_only=0&get_all_comments=1&no_reply_filter=1?r=US&IR=T

[xxi] http://www.kroll.com/en-us

[xxii] https://www.k2intelligence.com/en/

[xxiii] http://www.campaignlive.co.uk/article/sorrell-questions-us-media-agency-probe/1370527

[xxiv] http://www.ft.com/cms/s/0/13b31a4e-7bb4-11e5-98fb-5a6d4728f74e.html

[xxv] http://mediatel.co.uk/newsline/2015/11/02/schizoid-brands-media-agency-parsimony-vs-bond-profligacy/

[xxvi] #.uv3boe9vs

[xxvii] http://www.theguardian.com/artanddesign/gallery/2015/nov/30/anti-advertising-the-hijacked-bus-stops-of-paris-brandalism-climate-change-in-pictures?CMP=twt

www.ingramcontent.com/pod-product-compliance
Lightning Source LLC
Chambersburg PA
CBHW070234180526
45158CB00001BA/494